CORPORATE REALITIES

Corporate Realities focuses upon the human element in organisations. In describing the relations and actions which constitute every organisation (large or small) the authors assess the management issues and problems which invariably result. They demonstrate how the transition from small to large scale can be achieved, as well as reviewing recent attempts to recreate entrepreneurial forms of organisation in the context of larger, more complex ones. Finally, they examine the contrasting fortunes of various organisations in their attempt to adapt to the new economic and social conditions of the late 1990s.

In this way *Corporate Realities* opens a new agenda that captures the dynamic qualities of organisational life in both the large and small scale.

Robert Goffee is Professor of Organisational Behaviour at the London Business School.

Richard Scase is Professor of Organisational Behaviour at the University of Kent at Canterbury.

CORPORATE REALITIES

The dynamics of large and small
organisations

Robert Goffee and Richard Scase

INTERNATIONAL THOMSON BUSINESS PRESS
I ⓣ P An International Thomson Publishing Company

London • Bonn • Boston • Johannesburg • Madrid • Melbourne • Mexico City • New York • Paris
Singapore • Tokyo • Toronto • Albany, NY • Belmont, CA • Cincinnati, OH • Detroit, MI

Corporate Realities

 A division of International Thomson Publishing Inc.
The ITP logo is a trademark under licence

British Library Cataloguing-in-Publication Data
A catalogue record for this book is available from the British Library

First published by Routledge 1995
Simultaneously published in the USA and Canada by Routledge
Reprinted by International Thomson Business Press 1996

Typeset in Bembo by J&L Composition Ltd, Filey, North Yorkshire
Printed in the UK by T J International Ltd, Padstow, Cornwall

ISBN 0-415-05352-8 ✓

International Thomson Business Press
Berkshire House
168–173 High Holborn
London WC1V 7AA
UK

International Thomson Business Press
20 Park Plaza
13th Floor
Boston MA 02116
USA

http://www.thomson.com/itbp.html

CONTENTS

vi

ILLUSTRATIONS

FIGURES

CASE STUDY FIGURES

TABLES

CASE STUDY TABLES

CASE STUDIES

INTRODUCTION

There is no shortage of books on organisations. A number of standard texts cover the basics of organisational behaviour (Handy, 1993; Hales, 1993; Wilson and Rosenfeld, 1990; Hunt, 1992) and organisational structure (Butler, 1991; Mintzberg, 1983). The content of these suggests a remarkable consensus as to the core subject matter of organisational analysis – at least as far as the new student is concerned. Indeed, given only limited familiarity with the subject matter, it is possible to predict with some confidence – and not a little weariness – the contents pages of most American and British publications in this area. The best of these offerings provide a comprehensive overview of the major concepts and theories which have informed the study of organisations. In addition, they present useful summaries of the available research data which either confirm or question existing concepts and highlight the issues which require further investigation.

But there are a number of shortcomings. First, it is often the case that academic analysis is not easy to relate to everyday experience. Excessively abstract and 'neat' classifications of organisational structures, for example, fail because they underestimate – if not entirely discount – the people who inhabit and sustain them. This severely limits their potential to explain or predict actual behaviour. It also undermines their impact. What link, if any, exists between such analyses and the messy, apparently unpredictable, human actions and relationships which evolve within 'real' organisations? Few introductions to organisational behaviour seem able to capture the complexity or, indeed, the variety of organisational life.

To some extent, this latter shortcoming has been reinforced by the flood of publications over recent years which extol the virtues of high-performing organisations – as, for example, in the work of Kanter (1990) and Peters (1992). Much of this work is highly prescriptive and, in analytical terms, underdeveloped. Nevertheless, the almost obsessive interest in 'excellence' during the 1980s at least served to remind us that organisations consist of real people whose actions, relationships and attitudes fundamentally shape organisational capabilities. The problem, of course, is that most people live and work in organisations which are transparently *not* excellent – though some insiders (usually senior members) may publicly proclaim otherwise. For most, then, tales of excellence may be entertaining, and even inspirational, but they are, in a different way, as far removed from daily experience as more conventional organisational studies.

A second shortcoming of much textbook organisational analysis is its failure to capture the dynamic qualities of organisational life. Clearly, organisations experienced unprecedented levels of change during the 1980s and 1990s – much of it sudden and unpredictable. Dramatic shifts in the business environment – intensified (global) competition, technological change, currency fluctuation, deregulation, rapidly shifting consumer preferences – highlighted the need for new organisational capabilities. The requirements for cost effectiveness, and in many cases therefore, scale, were reinforced but at the same time there was a growing need for flexibility, responsiveness, innovation and quality. The search for these capabilities encouraged a shift towards looser, more organic forms of organisation. Large, integrated, hierarchically structured organisations began to fragment into flatter, market-focused, decentralised units. Organisational boundaries became increasingly difficult to delineate as closer relationships were established with, on the one hand, suppliers and subcontractors and, on the other, more quality-conscious customers.

Of course, the impact of these changes across different industries, economic sectors and countries varied significantly. Those who pronounced the death of bureaucracy, not for the first time, did so prematurely. Nevertheless, the transformation of structures, systems and, indeed, 'cultures' amongst a significant proportion of large-scale organisations – in both public and private sectors – was undeniable. (Scase and Goffee, 1989). In this context the presentation of organisational issues in many textbooks appears peculiarly dated – hardly surprising, perhaps, when some were originally published in the 1970s.

A third failing of conventional organisational studies is their almost exclusive focus upon large organisations. Given the virtually un-interrupted growth of both public and private large scale corpora-tions during most of the post-war period, this emphasis is understandable. But the 1980s were marked by a considerable resurgence of entrepreneurial activity and small-scale enterprise. The mix of factors driving this shift included increasing levels of unemployment; state subsidies for new business start-up; disillusion-ment with large-scale organisations; and a growing desire for auton-omy and the full utilisation of personal skills and abilities at work. As we conclude elsewhere,

> We see few indications that Britain and other Western countries will ever return to the 'good old days' of full employment. The increasing use of automated technology, the decline of labour-intensive industries and the growing competitive strength of manufacturing in developing countries will continue to 'de-industrialise' Western Europe and the United States and reduce the need for labour. There will, as a result, be a significant section of the potential labour force continually without jobs. At the same time there will be growing numbers of employees who are dissatisfied with their work in large corporations as they find themselves subject to tighter forms of managerial and tech-nological control. Accordingly, we envisage self-employment and business proprietorship as increasingly prevalent features of Western economies as they adapt to the post-industrial condi-tions of the late twentieth century.
>
> (Scase and Goffee, 1987a, pp. 165–6)

But the increased incidence of 'independent' business start-up only partially accounts for the resurgence of small-scale operations. As we discuss in the opening chapter, the strategic restructuring of *large-scale* organisations has also played a part. In order to maximise flexibility and minimise fixed costs many of these have subcontracted out operations previously conducted in-house. Others have facilitated 'spin-offs' and management buy-outs of non-core parts of their businesses. In some cases this process has been taken to such lengths that even some 'global' corporations have become little more than development and marketing 'shells' co-ordinating the efforts of myriad manufacturing units, distribution channels and sales outlets. Others have attempted to re-create the flexibility and responsiveness of small-scale organisation in-house through the establishment of relatively independent project teams, matrix structures, strategic business units and other organisational forms which maximise local operating autonomy and, in some cases, budget accountability.

Of all organisational types, we know least about these network structures and so-called 'adhocracies'. To some extent this is because they are new – at least within the context of larger organisations. They are also extremely complex and dynamic, so analysis is peculiarly difficult. As the same time, not much more is known about the organisational dynamics of 'independent' smaller-scale organisations. The assumption here seems to have been that they were becoming, at least until the 1980s, increasingly peripheral to the operation of modern, industrial economies. The fallacy of this view is apparent within both traditional (textiles, construction, retail) and modern (information technology, professional or 'knowledge intensive' services) sectors of industrialised economies. Yet despite their growing significance in the 1990s, we remain largely ignorant of the human and organisational issues which surround the formation and, in particular, the growth of smaller-scale organisations.

We have written this book on organisations in the hope that it might help overcome some of the deficiencies of existing texts. It is not, however, intended to compete with or replace standard introductions. Indeed, we have loosely adopted the model developed in Mintzberg's (1983) widely used text on organisational structure and processes. This specifies five key organisational co-ordinating mechanisms:

1 **Mutual adjustment**, where a pattern of co-ordination and communication unfolds informally as the work proceeds.
2 **Direct supervision**, where one person issues instructions to others and monitors their actions.
3 **Standardisation of work**, where tasks are tightly pre-specified in work rules and procedures and/or mechanised production processes.

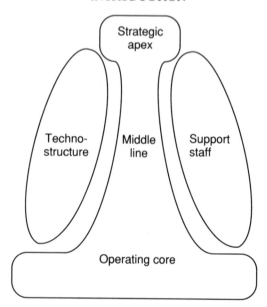

Figure I.1   Mintzberg's five parts of an organisation
Source: Mintzberg (1983, p. 11)

4 **Standardisation of outputs**, where work outcomes or results are specified through various performance measures.
5 **Standardisation of skills**, where, in the absence of precise or widely acceptable work or output standards, tasks are less directly co-ordinated through the internalised skills and knowledge of highly trained employees.

Mintzberg's analysis also distinguishes five component parts of an organisation (Figure I.1):

1 **The operating core**, which performs the basic work of producing goods and services by securing inputs, processing them and arranging for their distribution and sale.
2 **The strategic apex**, which has overall responsibility for formulating and implementing strategies designed to facilitate the achievement of organisational goals.
3 **The middle line** managers, who link the strategic apex to the operating core by managing information flows up and down the hierarchy and by directly co-ordinating the work of subordinates.

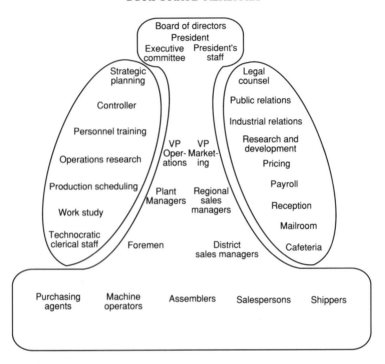

Figure I.2 Mintzberg's five basic parts of a manufacturing organisation
Source: Mintzberg (1983, p. 18)

4 **The technostructure**, which consists of analysts who set the standards relating to work processes, outputs and skills.
5 **The support staff**, who provide in-house, back-up services to other parts of the organisation.

As an example, the members and units of these five organisational components within a large-scale manufacturing business are shown in figure I.2.

As organisational scale and task complexity increase, there is a tendency to shift from the co-ordinating mechanisms of mutual adjustment and direct supervision to more standardisation. But in the most complex kinds of work, mutual adjustment amongst teams of experts becomes, once again, a key means of integration. These shifts impact upon the size and significance of the component parts and this, in effect, changes the shape of organisations. Linking co-ordinating mechanisms to organisational forms, Mintzberg thus differentiates the simple structure (direct supervision); the machine bureaucracy (standardisation of work); the professional bureaucracy (standardisation of skills); the divisional form (standardisation of outputs); and the adhocracy (mutual adjustment).

Clearly, however, few organisations fit neatly into one or other of these idealised types; most utilise a mix of co-ordinating mechanisms. Although, then, we apply some of the language of Mintzberg's model in this text, the associated series of relatively abstract organisational structures is not reproduced. Instead, the focus is upon more descriptive accounts of concrete experience within identifiable work settings. The significance of context – for example, industrial sector, labour markets and technology – is reflected in the organisation of chapters. Throughout we have attempted to give insight into the human relations and actions which constitute these organisations and the managerial issues which emerge from them. Our coverage, as the title implies, includes both large and small organisations. We examine the ways in which the transition from small to large scale can be managed and review recent attempts to recreate entrepreneurial forms of organisation within the context of large, complex organisations. Finally, we present contrasting pictures of the manner in which different organisations, large and small, have attempted – with varying degrees of success – to adapt to the contemporary economic and social conditions as we approach the year 2000.

1

THE TRADITIONAL ENTREPRENEURIAL FIRM

Until recently it would have been considered unusual to begin a book on organisational behaviour with a chapter on entrepreneurship. Traditionally, in management thinking, small businesses have been viewed as being of little importance in market economies largely dominated by large national and multinational corporations. In circumstances where such corporations can manipulate price levels, lobby governments and, both directly and indirectly, dictate market forces, the trading opportunities for small businesses would appear to be limited. Today, however, the attitude towards small businesses has changed.

In the conditions of the 1990s, small business and entrepreneurship are no longer seen as marginal to modern economies. Both government macroeconomic policies and corporate thinking now reflect small business values. Managers are encouraged to be entrepreneurial and to operate with structures which are flatter, with authority and responsibilities devolved to either cost or profit centres, business units and wholly-owned subsidiary companies. As such, corporate leaders are introducing organisational structures, cultures and operational practices which motivate managers to be more entrepreneurial in their day-to-day decision-making. They are trained to manage continuous change and are rewarded through performance-related results rather than through seniority-based promotion.

Opportunities for setting up profitable small business ventures are now greater than in the earlier post-war decades. Despite the growth of large corporations and their increasing market share, structural changes in modern economies are creating opportunities for small business growth (Dunne and Hughes, 1990). Corporate restructuring

1

is bringing about an increasing emphasis upon subcontracting and out-sourcing. As large organisations slim to their core activities to compete within specific market niches, they are buying in products and services. These can range from personnel development to accountancy support, secretarial assistance, transport, catering, equipment, maintenance, and to the purchase of semi-finished components (Wood, 1989). Through these changes, corporations are attempting to become more flexible in their trading by relying more upon market rather than employment relations as the underlying basis of their work processes. These changes have implications for business start-up in both manufacturing and service sectors. Because of the fragmentation of corporate activities, there are growing opportunities for both management buy-outs and management buy-ins. Equally, corporate out-sourcing is creating market niches for small entrepreneurial ventures which, because of their low overheads, are able to deliver, on a profitable basis, specialist goods and services. These trading arrangements offer continuing opportunities for business start-up and these trends have been reinforced by changes in the market place. The growth in affluence has created market niches for a wide range of personalised quality goods and services. Through patterns of personal expenditure, there is a growing tendency for consumers to express their individuality and differences in lifestyles. This provides a range of business opportunities for entrepreneurs able to meet specialist needs. Small business proprietors can carve out market niches in which they are able to trade profitably and, because of the personalised nature of the products and services, they can erect boundaries which restrict entry by larger competitors.

Such developments are part of broader socio-economic trends. Increasing affluence has led to greater purchasing of commodities and services associated with home maintenance, recreation and leisure, sport, physical fitness and various professional services. However, while some are small business proprietors for most of their working lives, others will engage in such activity for more limited periods. After pursuing careers in large corporations, or as a personal strategy to avoid unemployment, business start-up offers potentially attractive rewards. Accordingly, entrepreneurship is now more important than in the past, while equally, many medium-sized enterprises stem from very small-scale entrepreneurial origins.

WHY DO PEOPLE START THEIR OWN BUSINESSES?

The prime motive for business start-up is often viewed to be associated with financial reward. However, there are a range of factors, many of which stem from personal needs for independence and self-fulfilment. Many men and women choose to start their own businesses to escape from the controls, rules and regulations which are found in any employment relationship. They resent being told what to do by immediate bosses and object to their work patterns being regulated by organisational procedures. Business proprietors, despite their long working hours, the competitive threat of market forces, and the demands of their customers, can enjoy a greater degree of personal control in their relationships with others. Women in particular are attracted to entrepreneurship in the United States and Britain for this reason. Because of the nature of corporate cultures, career structures and managerial practices which often restrict their career advancement within various organisational settings, they stand to enjoy greater personal success and psychological autonomy through starting their own ventures. Equally, members of ethnic minorities can avoid prejudice and restricted career routes through business start-up.

The personal motives for business start-up will inevitably be a function of a variety of factors, of which psychological influences will play some role (See Figure 1.1). However, it has proven difficult to identify any particular characteristics of personality among those who start their own businesses (Chell, 1986). Social psychologists have searched for patterns, but their conclusions are contradictory and inconclusive. They tend to stress how, compared with others, entrepreneurs are more prone to take risks, to be innovative, and to search for personal autonomy in their working lives. However, such characteristics are ill-defined and insufficiently supported by scientific evidence (Kets de Vries, 1977). All that can be said about those who start their own businesses is that they are more able than others to work independently and to pursue their own economic

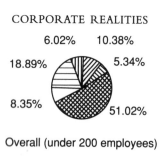

Overall (under 200 employees)

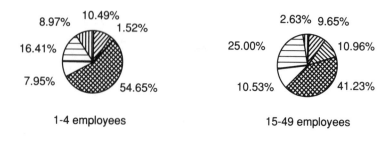

1-4 employees   15-49 employees

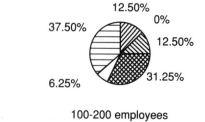

100-200 employees

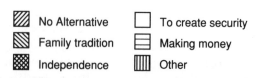

Figure 1.1 Motivations of small business proprietors in the United
Kingdom by size of firm
Source: Nat West Quarterly Survey of Small Businesses (QSSB), Vol. 6, No. 2, 1990

self-interest without the need for the structure and support systems
found in large organisations. In this sense, they tend to be 'inner-
directed' rather than 'outer-directed' in their patterns of behaviour
(Trompenaars, 1993). They have the confidence to establish a sense

of self-esteem which is independent of others' opinions. This 'inner locus of control' leads them to feel personally responsible for their own actions. This is in sharp contrast to others who are more inclined to develop social networks which are then significant in shaping feelings of self-respect. Entrepreneurs obtain self-esteem through their businesses, and accordingly the opinions of others are of limited importance. Interviews with those who have started their own businesses reveal a broad range of motives, attitudes and behaviour.

Motives for business start-up: some survey results

There is no clearly identifiable pattern. The motives for starting businesses are remarkably diverse among entrepreneurs. In the interviews there was a discrepancy between *general* notions about who starts businesses and the detailed accounts of their own *personal* histories. Although many subscribe to conventional notions about 'self-made' people, a totally different set of interpretations emerges in accounts of their own and other people's concrete experiences.

In our general conversations about the psychology of the business-owner, the same essential qualities are repeatedly emphasised. The owner-director of a company with 50 employees, for example, stressed the ability to ' . . . wrestle with any problem that comes along and to sort it out and to never give up. There's a certain will and determination to see the thing through – and to fight it all the way.' This is coupled with the qualities of *drive* and *ambition*. One of the small employers claimed that,

> You've got to be a bit more *ambitious* than your immediate counterparts. For a worker to set up on his own he has got to have a little more *ambition* than the worker on either side of him who's quite happy to plod. The most important quality that I've had to call upon myself has been my *resilience* and my *determination*. I think that just about covers everything for me. My *determination* makes me work hard when I'm tired. My *resilience* helps me to recover when I've had a terrible shock, when things have gone wrong.

But there was one further necessary quality – *independence*. This quality was strongly emphasised by an owner-director who argued that starting a business,

. . . attracts people who want to be their own boss, and for that reason often go ahead, and who have got a fair amount of *initiative* and who like to be *independent*. You don't get what I call the 'safety-first' type of chap, who goes into public service. It does tend to attract the type of chap who's got what I call sturdy *independence*.

But still these assumed psychological qualities do not complete the picture. Further capacities are emphasised; more specifically, reserves of *energy* and *enthusiasm* are regarded as particularly important. According to an owner-director, with an annual turnover of £6 million, 'It's got a lot to do with the amount of *energy* one's prepared to put into it. You put *energy* in the right direction and I think that the results are there.'

The motivation underlying the hard work and the risk that the 'self-made' man is prepared to take is seen by many as monetary gain. Comments emphasising the cash rewards of entrepreneurial risk were repeated many times, one of the more explicit being put forward by the owner of a company with a £100,000 turnover. He stated, 'I always think I'm going to make a fortune, and the day I stop thinking about it, I shall be lost.'

Personal satisfaction is acquired through developing a business rather than by enjoying a high personal standard of living. This is the picture of the business proprietor as conveyed by the interviews and it contains few surprises. He is seen to be hard working, ambitious, energetic and motivated by economic gain. This image has persisted over the decades, despite the dramatic changes which have occurred both within the economy and in the nature of business enterprises. Yet the whole picture is distorted by two fundamental flaws. First, ambitious, hard-working and energetic people are to be found in all walks of life and not solely among business proprietors. These notions, then, do not enable us to identify a distinguishable entrepreneurial type. Secondly, the image ignores a number of other important factors which are crucial in accounting for the *concrete* experiences of the people we interviewed.

When we turned from asking questions about the necessary personal qualities needed for business success *in general* to specific accounts of how they *actually* started their own enterprises, very different explanations were put forward. These were factual accounts within which there was no place for 'conventional wisdom' and received, everyday rhetoric. Analysis of these accounts indicates that many proprietors are

6

motivated by a wide range of social and non-economic factors of the sort that are often neglected in general discussions of entrepreneurial types. Thus, business formation and growth is often not the outcome of exceptional personal capacities of *drive*, *determination* and *ambition* but a function of various forms of personal discontent and random occurrence. Hence, for many of the people we interviewed, the reason for starting a business was not out of a desire ultimately to become a successful entrepreneur, but a *rejection* of working for somebody else. In rejecting the employee role, two major factors are emphasised – authority and the wage/profit relationship. For some, starting a business represents an escape from the control of others. As an owner with a turnover of £250,000 told us, 'I'm one of those people who find it very difficult to work under other people if I'm truthful. It's not something I do very well, put it that way. And that, amongst other things, is what made me start on my own.' Similarly, a self-employed man recalled, 'I was sort of an independent nature. Although I always got on alright working for people I was never particularly happy when I wasn't in charge of my own destiny.'

But there were others who felt that, as employees, they were being exploited. As one respondent recalled, 'I decided I was fed up with other people getting the money that I was really earning for them. They were all running about in fast cars and I was getting nothing.' If starting a business enables a person to escape from the constraints of authority, the wage/profit relationship and other features of being an employee, it also allows him or her to 'do a good job'. This was a factor in another respondents decision to 'go it alone'. 'I got fed up with being told how to do things which I knew were wrong. I had the manual skill and the technical ability to go on my own. That's the only way you can do what you want to do – to be on your own.' This statement was confirmed by a small employer who said, 'When I'm doing a job it's my decision and freedom as to whether I do it one way or another. Rather than worry about what some other chap wants me to do.' As employees, these men had felt they were unable to exercise their skills and they 'opted out' in order to produce good quality work. Such sentiments often persist long after the formation of a business. Although many of the people that we interviewed were motivated by economic gain, this was often bounded by the desire to produce 'a good job', 'something that is useful', 'something that the customer will be pleased with'.

These various examples do not deny that many businesses are set up with determinedly money-making motives but they do challenge the notion that every aspiring 'self-made' man glows with entrepreneurial fervour. It seems to us that the conventional view of the entrepreneurial type has serious shortcomings. It gives insufficient attention to the highly variable non-monetary factors that are often central to the formation of business enterprises and it imposes 'rational' and 'logical' explanations upon experiences and behaviour that are extremely diverse, personal and random. It is virtually impossible to predict those who will become entrepreneurs, business proprietors and 'self-made' men and yet the conventional wisdom persists.

Source: Scase and Goffee (1987a, pp. 29–37)

The motives underlying business start-up have important ramifications for the nature of business growth, their marketing strategies and their general style of management. It is too simplistic to collapse a diversity of proprietorial and managerial styles into a single generic category of 'small business' (Goss, 1991). The characteristics of skill, product and market are also important determining factors shaping significantly features of the management process within these firms. 'Low-skill', 'manual' or 'craft' enterprises will be organised rather differently from those providing professional services, or producing high-quality technological and scientific products. The rest of this chapter discusses the managerial characteristics of these *traditional* entrepreneurial firms; namely 'low-skill' and craft businesses (see Figure 1.2), while the next will consider the features of enterprises established on the basis of professional, technical and creative competences.

ORGANISATIONAL STRUCTURE AND MANAGEMENT STYLE

It is possible to differentiate small businesses according to the work and/or managerial roles of their proprietors. It is necessary to consider these before analysing the overall managerial issues of manual craft businesses in general.

Type (a): the self-employed

For many, self-employment is the ultimate goal of business proprietorship. Essentially, the self-employed undertake all tasks. They

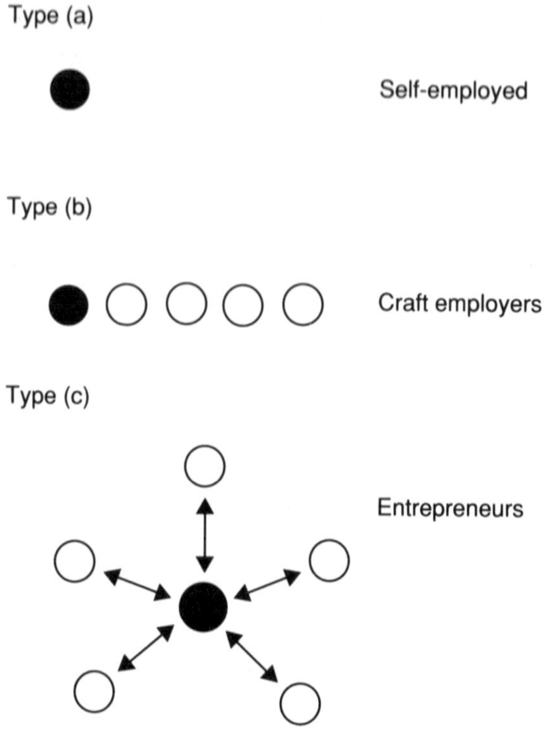

Type (a)

Self-employed

Type (b)

Craft employers

Type (c)

Entrepreneurs

Figure 1.2 The contrasting roles of traditional entrepreneurs

may make use of unpaid family labour or, at best, others on a part-time basis, but they employ no staff on a regular basis. Such businesses are usually set up on the basis of specific craft skills which are then used for the purposes of trading in a particular local market niche. These are the carpenters, plumbers, hairdressers, electricians, window cleaners, secretaries, car mechanics, and many others who sell to customers their personal skills of one kind or another. It is their detailed knowledge of trading opportunities within a particular locality that often motivates craft workers to start on their own. Their enterprises are based upon the delivery of goods and services to customers on a regular and personal basis. In this way, they have immediate feedback from the market in terms of response both to the quality of their services and to the prices which they charge.

Such traditional traders, however, often lack basic business manage-ment skills, since their overriding goal is to provide services to customers on the basis of their craft skills. For this reason they may under-charge, confuse turnover with profits, have high but hidden overheads and generally neglect the book-keeping and general administration of the business. It is weaknesses in these areas that lead to their high failure rates, particularly during recession as in the 1990s, rather than deterioration in the quality of services or products.

Self-employed enterprises often have precarious futures because they are entirely dependent upon the talents and energies of their proprietors, a feature which is reinforced by their reluctance to employ others. The latter is a function of their lack of management skills and training and also because of their underlying motive for business start-up – the need for personal independence. At the same time, their managerial weaknesses are often exposed in poor financial controls – inadequate monitoring of cash flow, pricing, and costs – and time management. They can under-estimate and, therefore, under-price their own time in their sale of goods and services. Many neglect market opportunities; instead, they choose to trade with a stable network of customers who will provide a regular and 'satisfactory' return on their efforts. They choose not to be profit-seekers, and theories of rational economic calculation cannot satisfactorily explain their behaviour (Scase and Goffee, 1987a).

Type (b): craft employers

Within traditional sectors of the economy – small-scale manufactur-ing, retailing and craft-based personal services – the self-employed often find that they are unable to meet the demands of their customers on the basis solely of their own skills, resources and time. It is necessary for them to hire employees on a more-or-less regular basis. Normally only two or three staff are employed, but it can be as many as twenty, depending upon the ability of the proprietor to manage as well as to work alongside them as a team member. In these businesses there is the emergence of a management function, since their proprietors have to organise the work process so that there are regular cash flows to pay wages and other costs associated with the employment of staff.

It is in businesses of this kind that the two basic principles of any organisation become apparent; those of integration and differentiation (Hunt, 1992). For self-employed proprietors the integration and division of work tasks is undertaken within the context of their own time management. Craft employers, by contrast, are faced with the need to break down and to differentiate business activities into specific job tasks and then integrate these through modes of personal supervision and control. How is this undertaken within businesses which employ no more than five or six people? If in large organisations some type of division of labour is more-or-less taken for granted, and is embedded within structures of authority and responsibility, this is less so in small businesses, with the result that the allocation of duties is always more uncertain, variable and problematic. Accordingly, the division of tasks and the specification of jobs is the outcome of a process of *mutual adjustment*. The division and integration of the work process is based upon the interdependence of employees undertaking duties in a flexible and broadly-defined manner. This can be a source of employee work satisfaction because the delineation of job duties through mutual adjustment offers task variety which may not be available within the more bureaucratised structures of many large organisations. Mutual adjustment also binds individuals into teams, with the result that a high premium is attached to personal compatibilities between employer and employees as well as among employees themselves. Equally there is the need for high-trust relations since, without these, mutual adjustment as an organising process is unlikely to generate productive and profitable business performance.

It is for this reason that staff recruitment is a psychologically delicate and complex process in small firms. It is not a matter simply of selecting employees according to their technical competences; the extent to which they will fit into teams and contribute to harmonious interpersonal relations must also be considered. Because of the need for high trust in sustaining processes of mutual adjustment, there is a tendency for proprietors to select their employees from family members, long-term friends and acquaintances, and this can lead them to give secondary importance to skills and competences. Recruitment is often a compromise between competence and compatibility and it can be a source of considerable tension within many small businesses. Rarely are personal compatibilities and expert skills perfectly matched and the former may be given priority over the latter in the small business proprietor's recruitment process.

A feature of traditional craft-based enterprises managed on the basis of mutual adjustment is the absence of a distinctively separate management function and the exercise of authority through formal hierarchical control. Relatively low profit margins prevent proprietors withdrawing from the performance of productive work tasks and becoming full-time managers and supervisors of others. They, themselves, are part of the process of mutual adjustment and as such, they are members of teams working alongside their employees. It is through this involvement that they fulfil the managerial function. Instead of issuing instructions, they determine the criteria for quality and quantity of employee performance through personal example. As such, proprietorial authority is exercised *within* rather than superimposed *upon* the work process. This reaffirms the need for personal compatibility between employers and employees and the vital importance of high-trust relationships. Within these, proprietors have to maintain a delicate balance between their identification with employees' interests, and the distance needed to fulfil the proprietorial function.

It is because of a lack of clearly-defined work roles and procedures that such businesses can give the impression of being poorly managed. But this, in fact, can be a major strength of businesses managed on the basis of mutual adjustment. Their organisation in flexible teams is often a major reason for high employee morale, motivation and commitment. Further, there can hardly be a more effective method of monitoring staff in terms of the quality and quantity of their performance than by working alongside them on a day-to-day basis.

The major weakness of managing small businesses according to this method, is that it is not conducive to growth. Since team relationships are carefully nurtured around networks of specific, highly compatible individuals, any increase in staff numbers can destroy the productive and profitable interpersonal dynamics of the business. At the same time, by co-ordinating work activities through processes of mutual adjustment, proprietors fail to develop the managerial competences necessary for running larger businesses.

These more explicit methods of formal control may be necessary to manage growth and larger businesses.

Many key features of the management process within traditional entrepreneurial businesses are illustrated in the following description of a small engineering firm.

Hill Enterprises

When Hill Enterprises was founded ten years ago, its total assets consisted of one automatic lathe, one contract worth £2,200, and one employee. The employee was Robert Hill, proprietor and sole owner, then twenty-nine years old. He had one objective in forming Hill Enterprises – that of retiring with a million pounds in his personal bank account at the age of forty.

According to Robert Hill, the reasons Hill Enterprises was able to survive the first difficult years were his considerable abilities as a machinist, which he had developed during the nine years he was employed in the machine shop of a large manufacturing company, his willingness to work long and hard hours, and his knack for raising money for working capital. During the early years, he would customarily spend his evenings working at the plant and his days visiting banks, insurance companies, and personal friends in an attempt to acquire sufficient funds to continue operations. For the most part he was successful, and though he often had the feeling that he was a bit over-extended financially, his business continued to grow and to show profits.

Mr Hill felt that another reason for his success was his ability to inspire the workforce to work toward his personal goal of a million pounds. His typical comment in interviewing a prospective employee was: 'If you work for me you will have to work hard, for I intend to retire with a million pounds by the time I am forty. This means overtime, long hard hours, and unswerving loyalty to Hill Enterprises. If you are willing to do this I'll make sure that you will get your share of the profits.'

Potential employees who were willing to accept these conditions found that Mr Hill meant what he said. Loyalty to the common cause was based on the number of hours of overtime a man put in. This high amount of overtime had two effects. First, Hill Enterprises was able to give its employees approximately double the take-home pay they could receive from other companies, thus reinforcing the promises Mr Hill had made concerning financial rewards to individual employees. Second, even though the company was constantly growing and the workforce was increasing in size, the large amount of overtime kept the number of employees to a minimum so that Mr Hill had continuing face-to-face contact with them and could maintain a personal relationship with each of the men.

As Hill Enterprises grew and progressed, Robert Hill continued his earlier pattern of operations. He set a gruelling pace, continuing to work long hours late into the night and spending a large share of his time during the day attempting to raise additional working capital and financial support. He often held important conferences at 5.00pm in order that supervisory personnel would be free to handle their regular work during the 'normal' working hours. Mr Hill seemed to enjoy the pace and pressure and seemed especially to like his frequent contact with the employees. His office consisted of a single desk in one corner of the production area. Thus he was immediately available to all to help with any problem, whether a production or a personal one. Many employees availed themselves of his accessibility and while he was in the plant he seemed to be constantly talking with one employee or another, either in his 'office' or on the production floor. Often he would report on the progress of his financial affairs to the men, a practice which they enjoyed tremendously, as Mr Hill would recount very vividly his financial manipulations.

The employees of Hill Enterprises responded to the situation by working long hours in poor environmental surroundings and under the constant pressure of schedules and production deadlines. Hill Enterprises had at this stage set up operations in a deserted store building, and physical working conditions were considerably less attractive than those of competing organisations.

Under the constant pressures to meet schedules, tempers were often short. The accepted way to reduce individual tension was to 'fly off the handle'. It was the privilege of the Director as well as of any employee, and it was a privilege that was often used. Robert Hill had the reputation of being able to deliver the best 'dressing-down' of anyone in the organisation, and it was not unusual for an employee to comment on the skill with which Mr Hill had 'chewed him out'. This situation was not all one-sided and employees, regardless of their position, felt free to talk back to Mr Hill or the other supervisors and often did. And because this was the accepted way to decrease tension and to achieve action, the incident over which an outburst occurred was immediately for-gotten. The employees seemed to enjoy their existence with Hill Enterprises and underneath the tension and pressure each employee felt that he was capable, and that he was contributing to the goals of the company.

Source: London Business School case study

Small businesses, organised on a basis of such informal mechanisms, have to undergo a process of organisational restructuring if they are to grow. It is generally necessary for proprietors to cease working alongside their staff and instead to become more fully occupied with the administration of their businesses. As a result, the management function is undertaken by proprietors through various face-to-face mechanisms of direct control.

Type (c): entrepreneurs

These owner-managers exercise control over their businesses through directly imposed but mostly unwritten guidelines and instructions. They may employ up to fifty or sixty staff, but it can be far greater, depending on the ability of proprietors to exercise control through informal, face-to-face processes rather than according to formalised structures and job descriptions. Unlike craft employers, they do not rely upon establishing performance criteria through personal example. Although in the larger of these enterprises there may be supervisors and managers, the exercise of authority and responsibility is concentrated in their proprietorial hands. By dint of ownership, proprietors possess legitimacy to impose business decisions, often in a more-or-less arbitrary manner. They may consult with key employees, but typically they retain almost total control and remain at the centre of the decision-making web.

In these enterprises a high premium is attached to nurturing strong but informal cultures. Employee integration tends to be on the basis of personal allegiance to proprietors. Such enterprises are structured around the 'personalities' of their owner-managers and their growth potential is highly dependent upon proprietors' preferences, energies, and plans. The presence or absence of children or of other family members who may be interested in taking over the business will often determine whether or not the enterprise expands, rather than considerations associated with product development, profit optimisation and market opportunities. Accordingly, rational decision-making within entrepreneurial enterprises is often bounded by, or contingent upon, a range of sentimental and personal factors. It is for such reasons that these businesses can be highly vulnerable with their financial viability intricately interwoven with the talents, energies and the personalities of their proprietors.

Leadership and the small firm

The structure of this sort of company is (very) simple. Organizational schemes hardly exist and there are relatively few explicit rules and procedures. Tasks are allocated directly by the founder-owner or by close associates. Mutual collaboration is great; coordination is achieved largely by mutual agreement. The final criterion in problem-solving situations is 'what would the boss think we should do?'. There are few staff departments in this sort of company. Such as they are, they are preferably kept as small as possible. They are seen rather as a necessary evil than as an indispensable good.

The culture is a 'family culture' presided over by the 'father'. The dominant norm is loyalty and dedication, more so than performance and success with clients. Flexibility, mutual helpfulness, informality and devotion are key words.

Status and position are relatively unimportant except of course for the one at the top; but that position and its status are also practically unassailable. For the rest of the staff, loyalty, discipline, specialized competence and fitting in with the 'family' are what counts. Handy typifies this culture as a power culture.

The strategies of these companies are determined by 'the boss'. Strategies develop to a great extent intuitively and by trial and error. They have a relatively short time-span and are mostly focus strategies.

The boss or bosses at the top are more leaders than managers. Their leadership is based on power plus either charisma and/or professional expertise. Their style of leadership is dominated by two extremes: on the one hand 'telling', that is to say, stating without much explanation what is required and how; on the other hand complete delegation, which is naturally only used with employees who enjoy complete confidence.

These companies do particularly well in a rapidly expanding, often not too easy, but not unfriendly market.

Source: Swieringa and Wierdsma (1992, pp. 47–8)

Within the context of direct, face-to-face relations with staff and in the absence of formalised rules and procedures, owner-managers develop a number of strategies for cultivating employee commitment (Scase and Goffee, 1982). The most common of these is the appeal of *charisma*. Some proprietors nurture business cultures which serve to exaggerate their own extraordinary qualities and, through this, they link their own achievements with those of their business and, equally important, with their employees. In this way, proprietors appeal to their staff to exercise exceptional commitment and output in return for generous financial rewards. Sometimes this can be in the form of overtime or, more usually, through year-end bonuses, sales commissions, and profit-related payment systems. Since these rewards are offered within the context of highly personalised, informal face-to-face relations – in sharp contrast to the working procedures of large bureaucratic organisations – they serve to reinforce employee allegiance to, and their dependency upon, their employers. In the deliberate absence of formalised rules and guidelines, such rewards are always discretionary and may be seen as an attempt by proprietors to legitimate their control through the maintenance of dependency relations. This can be particularly effective if employees are low-skilled and have competences which are only relevant within the context of their proprietors' enterprises. In lacking transferable skills, they become excessively dependent upon their continuing personal compatibility with their employers.

An alternative for proprietors is to exercise control through more *paternalistic* methods. As such, they attach considerable importance to the social as well as the economic responsibilities of being 'local' employers who share the long-term interests of their staff. As with charismatic strategies, the intended outcome is a high level of employee dependency, underwritten by employers' discretionary use of material rewards and fringe benefits.

Alongside these two proprietorial styles, there is the classic *autocratic* approach, whereby entrepreneurs manage their staff in a more impersonal, calculative and instrumental manner (Scase, 1995). Owners stress the purely economic character of their businesses and the fact that, in order to survive, and for jobs to be preserved, wage costs must be kept to a minimum. As a result, working conditions are often poor, rates of pay are low and there is a high level of staff turnover. This autocratic style tends to be found where the nature of the product or service requires very low employee skills and where labour market conditions enable staff to be readily hired and fired as well as being employed irregularly or on a part-time basis. It is a method of management which leads to low employee trust and which exploits and reinforces the vulnerability and dependence of unskilled labour. Such a proprietorial style is often found in the hotel and catering, cleaning, textile and clothing, and subcontracted low-skill, machine tool industries. Although the above styles – charismatic, paternalistic, and autocratic – can be considered as distinctive, they are often juxtaposed with each other within the same small business. Proprietors will often use a variety of interpersonal techniques, drawing upon each of them in relation to different categories of employees. For example, the paternalistic style may be applied to long-term, relatively indispensable employees, whilst the autocratic approach may be reserved for temporary, less skilled workers.

Within such enterprises, there is often greater clarity and specification of work tasks than is found within smaller craft employer businesses. If in the latter, processes of mutual adjustment determine the allocation of job duties, the proprietors of entrepreneurial firms manage through mechanisms of direct control, devoting more attention to setting up explicit systems of responsibility and control. Even so, the division of work and associated job descriptions remain relatively loose compared with those found in many larger organisations.

The characteristics of these entrepreneurial enterprises enable them to have many strengths in relation to larger, competitive organisations. The centralised authority vested in proprietors enables there to be rapid strategic decision-making with a minimum degree of employee consultation. Accordingly, these businesses can be very adaptive, swiftly adjusting their trading capacities according to changing market opportunities. Further, by managing through direct face-to-face supervision, owners are able to monitor employee performance closely, and to exercise tight controls over operating costs. However, the potential of these strengths can be untapped because of other inherent weaknesses associated with the indispensable roles of their proprietors. Even if there are managers and others who undertake some of the supervisory tasks, systems of delegation in terms of responsibility, authority and decision-making usually remain underdeveloped. This is often because of the predominant power cultures of these businesses. In the absence of formalised systems, the management function is exercised by owners developing networks of personal allegiance. Within cultures which stress the importance of employee compliance, decision-making is rarely queried or subject to detailed employee scrutiny. Employees may be powerless as their employers take decisions which can jeopardise the future viability of the business.

Equally, weaknesses in systems of delegation are conducive to proprietors becoming overburdened with work and responsibilities. This can lead to impaired decision-making and to proprietors becoming preoccupied with day-to-day operational matters, rather than with longer-term strategic issues. The outcome can be weak business planning and a failure to respond to, and take advantage of, changing market opportunities. Consequently, the potential to exploit the flexible advantages of their small businesses is not fully realised because of owner-managers' reluctance to delegate, their operational overload, and the lack of time which they devote to monitoring market trends and changing customer preferences.

The proprietors of these small businesses often fail to set up adequate financial controls, there being a tendency for costs to grow and for cash flow to be confused with profits. As a result, the relative cost advantages of small businesses can be under-realised because of weaknesses in financial management. This often stems from their background and experience, since although they may be good entrepreneurs, they often have weaknesses as managers (Slatter, 1992). Indeed, the qualities required for the former are often quite distinct from those needed for the latter. They are often independently-minded and committed to the pursuit of personal goals, with a tendency to ignore the advice of others. Management, on the other hand, requires an ability to operate within structures whereby human, financial and technical resources are utilised. It is necessary for them to delegate and to devise effective procedures for the division and integration of work processes, so that goals are achieved. Often entrepreneurs are reluctant to develop such skills, with the consequence that successful business start-up can be followed by failure because, with growth, they lack the necessary management competences.

Such problems can be compounded by a lack of management depth in entrepreneurial ventures. Proprietors' reluctance to delegate may lead to the under-development of management skills among staff and the under-utilisation of their talents and skills. This can be a deliberate strategy which facilitates the retention of tight control over business operations with little challenge to proprietorial authority. However, businesses become over-dependent upon proprietors and, at the same time, staff may become disaffected and de-motivated. Further, little attention is often given to management succession, with the effect that the longer-term future of such businesses is uncertain. They can be so dependent upon the health and energies of their proprietors that, without the development of effective management systems, owners' retirement can lead to businesses ceasing to trade.

Traditional entrepreneurial enterprises, then, are always precarious, with their viability dependent not only upon changes in market conditions and customer preferences, but also the talents and energies of their proprietors. By nurturing cultures and structures which sustain their own indispensability, these business owners sow the seeds not only for successful short-term growth but also – paradoxically – for their potential failure. Because small businesses as a whole lack formalised management structures and since, in essence, they constitute little more than informal networks of personal face-to-face relations, it is hardly surprising that so few acorns mature into fully-grown oak trees. But this, perhaps, is a necessary feature of modern economies. As market niches and opportunities for business start-up change, the composition of the small business sector continually revitalises itself. This is certainly the case in the more traditional manual sectors where businesses are set up on the basis of proprietors' craft skills. But increasingly businesses are being set up by those who have managerial, professional and high-level technical competences and who are trading in the newly-emerging market niches of what are rapidly becoming post-industrial economies. The characteristics of these are discussed in the next chapter.

ORGANISATIONAL ISSUES

For the self-employed, the key managerial issues are those to do with effective time management and the ability to acquire the financial and marketing skills necessary for the efficient sale of their craft and technical-based competences. For those wishing to expand their volume of trading so that the hiring of staff becomes essential, it is important to be able to delegate duties and to monitor the performance of others. With further expansion of their businesses, proprietors have to acquire a broad range of interpersonal skills whereby they are able to handle the restructuring of 'team' dynamics, and employer–employee relations that are required as job duties become allocated to a growing number of staff. Without such skills, processes of mutual adjustment can be threatened and with this, the longer-term viability of the business jeopardised.

2

MANAGING THE CREATIVE AND PROFESSIONAL SMALL BUSINESS

Growing numbers of managers, technologists, highly-qualified specialists and professionals are leaving the relative security of the corporation to risk starting up their own businesses. Many of them feel that their personal talents and skills are not being fully utilised. Middle-aged managers often accept redundancy and experiment with entrepreneurship, often with initial financial support from their previous employers. Younger managers, on the other hand, who have been encouraged to expect opportunities for creativity, challenge and self-fulfilment in their jobs, are often disappointed. Consequently, they are increasingly convinced that entrepreneurship may offer an alternative route for the achievement of such goals. Some of the emerging patterns are described in the following extract, which summarises attitudes in a recent survey of managers.

The creative and professional enterprise: why men start businesses

Our survey covered 324 male managers, aged 25–65, in six large organisations. It is often said that when managers give up corporate jobs to start their own businesses, they are opting out: running guest houses in the West Country, teashops in Sussex and garden centres in East Anglia. This is not the case – at least, not among the managers in the survey. On the contrary, they were attracted to starting businesses which would use their work-based skills and exploit the talents acquired in their corporate jobs. In fact, their major motive for starting businesses is to use their management skills more fully. More than 20 per cent feel their companies are not making the best use of their managerial talents, and of these, two-thirds are thinking of setting up their own businesses.

This response suggests that many corporations are wasting managerial talent on a wide scale, which presumably has considerable repercussions on their financial performance.

The sort of manager who wants to start his own business has a strong need for self-fulfilment, creativity and opportunities for independent judgement. It is because the need isn't met that such people want to start their own businesses. Frustrations at work are often directed towards the immediate boss: of managers dissatisfied with their boss, no fewer than 75 per cent had considered business proprietorship. Other motivators include the fact that 'the cost of career pursuit greatly outweighs the benefits', 'employment inhibits personal growth', and 'small-scale organizations are more satisfying places to work than large ones.'

These managers are not dissatisfied with the work itself; it is the organisational conditions which frustrate them. Two-thirds of those considering a business start-up see work (rather than family or leisure pursuits) as the major source of personal satisfaction in their lives. For most managers, proprietorship is a vehicle for opting in rather than out, an opportunity to pursue work more fully.

Many possess some of the key skills required for starting commercial ventures: for example, detailed knowledge of specific markets, particular products and services, financial management, staff supervision, and so on. What they lack are some basic, but easily acquired, business techniques needed at start-up: for example, cash flow forecasting, viability analysis, commercial negotiation, raising finance.

Business start-ups are currently concentrated in the retail and service sectors – restaurants, garden centres, consultancies, shops, professional services, etc. Our survey suggests that managers want to start businesses on the basis of their work-related skills – particularly those employed in traditional manufacturing and high technology. Many have ideas about how they could create manufacturing facilities which are technically more efficient than those which they are currently using. Others could identify highly profitable niches in the market.

Source: Scase and Goffee (1987b)

Despite the appeals of corporate leaders for middle managers to take initiatives and to be more 'proactive', many aspects of organisational change are restricting their working autonomy. The increasing application of management information systems, tighter budgetary controls, and the slimming down of management tiers are putting many middle managers under closer scrutiny. Although they are encouraged to be more innovative, their hands are tied and economic conditions lead them to be risk-adverse. The outcome is job dissatisfaction, leading older managers to take early retirement and encouraging many of their younger colleagues to consider business start-up, freelancing and self-employment (Scase and Goffee, 1989).

These patterns are not confined to men; more women with professional qualifications are being appointed to management positions but their ambitions are often frustrated because of the reality of corporate life. The nature of corporate cultures, stipulating notions of managerial effectiveness, often undervalues their competences (Davidson and Cooper, 1992). They often feel passed-over for promotion and as a result seek to pursue their careers through entrepreneurial ventures. This accounts for the growing proportion of businesswomen in Europe and North America.

The creative and professional enterprise: why women start businesses

Many women claim they started their own businesses because of various unsatisfactory experiences associated with being employees. More specifically, proprietorship offers an opportunity to escape from employer- and managerial-imposed control systems of the work place. Here, there are parallels with the motives of men who start their own businesses because they want to obtain a greater degree of personal working autonomy.

'I didn't want to work for anybody else. I like the freedom of running my own business. When you're working for other people you could really work hard . . . and get no credit for it. Then, the minute you ease up . . . everyone's down on you like a ton of bricks.'

'I was totally at the mercy of other people's whims and fancies . . . I suddenly thought I would set up on my own. I thought I couldn't possibly make a worse hash of my life than everybody else was making for me . . . I'd had it working for other people. I was either going to be a wage slave for the rest of my life or be entirely my own boss . . . (Now) I love not having anyone telling me what to do.'

25

The interviews suggest that one of the major reasons why these women had started their own businesses is because of limited career prospects in large-scale organisations. In other words, they regard entrepreneurship as a means for obtaining economic and personal success because of the inability to fulfil ambitions within more conventional career structures. The overwhelming majority of the women are university graduates who have been employed in a variety of middle-management positions. They feel their career prospects are limited because of the existence of various gender-related prejudices.

> 'I'm quite ambitious. I want to do various things with my life . . . But in my last job there was no future in it. I set up this business because I was fed up with people saying "Are you thinking of getting married?", or "Are you having a child?". I got sick to death of it. Never got anywhere. Well, I thought, I don't have to put up with this. Who needs to? If you set up something on your own, as long as you survive, you don't have to listen to that. I love not having all those office politics. I just get on with the job.'

> 'After I got married, I announced to the Board that I was going to have a baby . . . They refused to accept that I wanted to come back as managing director of their market research subsidiary. They brought in somebody over me, and demoted me to director even though I was back at work after two months . . . They would not accept that you can be a managing director as well as a working mother. This resistance and totally stupid attitude meant an important turning point for me. I felt desperately I could do it better . . . just as simple as that. I got fed up being employed. I wanted to be an employer . . . I wanted autonomy, to be able to run my own business.'

> 'I worked my way up through British publishing and became an assistant editor in a literary agency . . . I walked out of that agency which I worked for because they said I was no good. That gave me the incentive . . . I had to extend myself . . . I started my own agency . . . I knew I was every bit as bright and successful as my male contemporaries, many of whom are still stuck in their jobs . . . I just wanted to make money for myself. I was certain I could put my talents into developing my own business . . . I'm pretty creative and I'm very energetic.'

These women are typical of those who opt out of careers in large corporations because they resent working for other people. In this they share a common motive with a large number of male proprietors who also start their own businesses because they are not prepared to adhere to the supervision and control of others. This, together with a general resentment of making profits for owners and shareholders, is a major reason why both men and women start their own businesses. For some, such businesses provide a means for 'getting by' and obtaining a satisfactory standard of living through trading in the market. Thus, for them, business survival and market stability is their major concern. But with others, there is a long-term commitment to business growth as a means of acquiring an ever-increasing level of personal success. Despite their frustrated careers, the women we interviewed had not rejected the success goals of modern society or the values associated with the work ethic. On the contrary, entrepreneurship was seen by them to be an alternative route for achieving the same goals. Indeed, for some of them it was seen to offer a strategy whereby hard work and endeavour could be better rewarded. As a result, they were usually preoccupied with running their own businesses to the extent of sacrificing almost everything else. Their personal identities were almost entirely tied up with the success and failure of their businesses and in this they expressed some of the more extreme features of psychological immersion that is so typical of successful male entrepreneurs.

Source: Goffee and Scase (1985, pp. 41, 62–3)

What kinds of businesses do former corporate managers set up? It is often in their capacity as corporate specialists of one kind or another that they have been able to identify market trends and to determine, within these, niches for trading opportunities. It is not unusual for managers to negotiate deals with their previous employers' customers to give them their first trading opportunities and with these, to raise finance. In common with traditional craft entrepreneurs, their businesses are often highly dependent upon their own particular talents and skills. It is with these that products and services are traded.

The growth of these businesses has been most pronounced in those economic sectors where there has been corporate fragmentation, down-sizing and associated processes of out-sourcing. The media offer many examples of these trends, with more than one-half of those working in this sector being freelance, self-employed or the proprietors and partners of small business enterprises. Television broadcasting companies, for example, now purchase programmes from producers and directors who in turn hire, on a project and temporary basis, freelance sound engineers, camera crews, and other staff. The television industry, once integrated on the basis of large corporations with both in-house production and broadcasting functions, has become an example of the 'virtual' corporation, fragmented around a network of broadcasters who are little more than commissioning agents of programmes made by small-scale enterprises.

A similar process is occurring within other media sectors such as newspaper, magazine and book publishing, advertising and the performing arts. Out-of-house freelance specialists are commissioned to contribute to specific projects which are co-ordinated by their clients. Areas of London, New York, Paris and other capital cities are taking on the features of closely knit occupational districts where networks of independent specialists are constantly grouping and re-grouping to offer contractual services to commissioning clients. Equally, the financial services sector has become fragmented around a core of major insurance companies, finance houses and other banking institutions. Self-employed consultants and advisers, operating from home-based work stations, increasingly 'interface' between the purchasers and suppliers of corporate services. Often partnerships and small limited companies, offering specialist financial services within precisely-designated market niches, are set up.

Increasing affluence and the greater disposable income of the middle classes in Europe and the United States offer opportunities for business start-up among corporate managers and others with specialist skills in finance, investment and accountancy. There are also growing business opportunities for those occupying middle-level management positions possessing specialist skills associated with new technology, telecommunications, and information systems. Demands for software and computer packages have generated a sector of small-scale providers who prefer to be self-employed rather than to work in large corporations. Many university graduates with such skills obtain work experience in large companies before moving on to smaller software houses or setting up their own businesses, often in partnership with like-minded others. Similarly, more sophisticated consumer markets have led to the growth of public relations, promotion and marketing functions which, instead of being undertaken in-house, are out-sourced to freelance specialists who often pool their personal talents. How, then, are these enterprises managed and what are their organisational characteristics?

ORGANISATIONAL STRUCTURE AND MANAGEMENT STYLE

The organisation of work on the basis of specialist and changing customer needs tends to produce 'flexible' work roles, duties and responsibilities. Instead of the performance of routine tasks, adaptiveness and job variety are the predominant characteristics of these enterprises. Equally, their small-scale nature means that little can be offered to employees in the form of conventional promotion prospects. If these are important sources of motivation for managers in large organisations, they are generally absent within small firms. In the latter, psychological rewards are obtained through personal *self-fulfilment* and individual *recognition*. This has ramifications for management styles, interpersonal relations between proprietors and employees, business cultures and structures, and growth strategies (Slatter, 1992). Work roles tend to be broadly defined with high levels of discretion and responsibility. Professional employees working in these small businesses are assumed to prefer personal autonomy, responsibility and recognition and, indeed, these are typically their motives for moving from employment in large organisations. Staff are encouraged to develop close working relationships with clients so that in a relatively autonomous manner, they can exercise particular expert, creative and technical skills.

Personal recognition is also an important reward because of the significance of broader 'professional' reference groups. In advertising, television, film, the performing arts, and public relations, there are numerous rewards and other tokens of recognition that constitute important motivators for those working in these industries. Equally, professional bodies stipulate standards of conduct and criteria for terms of trade which shape relationships between the buyers and sellers of services. It is only in the consideration of these factors that it is possible to understand the internal dynamics and the management processes of these creative and professional businesses. The demands of employees for continuous challenge and self-development are illustrated in the case below.

Secure Systems

Bill had joined Secure Systems ten months ago. He had come from a major software house and had been excited to join a fast growing computer security company with an impressive image in the market.

'With the Data Protection Act coming into operation this year, lots of organizations are starting to get very worried about the security of their computer systems, Bill', explained Rod Thomas, the Managing Director, after Bill had his successful selection interview. 'One particular client, Gremlin Geotronics, does an awful lot of work for the Ministry of Defence, and for them, of course, security is the name of the game. I'd like you to start here by going over Gremlin's systems, making recommendations to their board, and implementing the new high-security systems in line with their requirements.'

This was quite a feather in Bill's cap, his creative genius was being recognized. At his previous job he had shown innovative ability, but the company was quite bureaucratized, and he had felt stifled in that sort of climate. Certainly, he had had a good salary – Secure Systems weren't paying him any more – a pleasant office and good secretarial back-up, but he felt restricted and he had steadily got more frustrated. The chance to move to Secure Systems was just what he had been waiting for.

Over the next eight months he put his heart and soul into the Gremlin project. Most of that time he had worked at Gremlin Geotronics sites anyway, only coming back to his office for a few weeks at a time to revise and consolidate systems designs and to catch up with his mail. He had struck up a friendship with Leslie Jones, a computer analyst who shared his office, and who had a dry, sardonic sense of humour. Leslie made Bill feel slightly uncomfortable at times.

'Bet you never thought you'd have to share a little box like this when you came here, eh, Bill?' Leslie remarked ironically as Bill shifted one box of printouts to get at some papers below it. 'Beats me why you put up with it: after all, I'm only one of the juniors here, not like you. You must be on at least £5000 a year more than me.'

Bill flustered, 'Well, it's the challenge, Leslie. This project is so fascinating and it's posing all sorts of problems that I like to solve. I think also that some of the new ideas I've got are transferable, in that we'll be able to use them as a basis for work in other companies. Come on, Leslie, it's the work which turns me on, not where I do it!'

After eight months the Gremlin Geotronics project was finished, and Bill Johnson was mostly office-based for the next two months. There was no immediate project to follow the Gremlins one, and Bill got locked into a standard office routine, dealing with small jobs as they turned up, and trying to do some development work in his spare time. Leslie's mannerisms and cynical, cutting humour began to get on his nerves. With time on his hands, Bill started to take notice of his surroundings.

Source: Ludlow (1987, pp. 3–4)

Even though the creative energies of employees are the major asset of such businesses, and the need for self-fulfilment must be addressed, there must also be suitable financial rewards. However, the discretionary nature of work means that pay and performance can rarely be precisely measured. Further, the organisation of work activities around client-determined projects can entail the cultivation of long-term relationships with financial returns accruing over relatively lengthy periods of time. Employees, then, often expect to have a financial stake in the future of their businesses, since the assets are largely comprised of their own and their colleagues' expert skills. Hence, enterprises that trade with creative and expert skills are often set up as *partnerships* rather than as sole proprietorships. A further reason for the partnership form is that previously disaffected colleagues may, together, possess complementary skills for start-up. Similarly, partnerships offer support systems and shared competences which reduce the risks inherent in business start-up. But more important is the fact that such partnerships enable individuals whose skills are indispensable for business success to have a stake in ownership. Although partners may pay themselves relatively low wages in the short-term, they enjoy longer-term benefits in the incremental increases in the value of their businesses. Ownership stakes are often extended to those employees who demonstrate high commitment and performance; equally, new staff are often attracted by this promise. In these ways participation in ownership is a means for incentivising colleagues in enterprises where staff skills provide the basis for value-added trading. Without such arrangements, tensions can easily emerge, leading to staff resenting the fact that their talents and skills are being exploited by others for personal gain.

If the underlying principles of any organisation, whether large or small, are those of integration and differentiation, within these businesses tendencies to differentiation can dominate. Again, partnerships offer an appropriate solution, since sources of individualism, division and segmentation within work processes are compensated by the integrative mechanism of joint ownership. But the tendency to differentiation makes these businesses prone to break-up, with partners selling their stakes to set up their own ventures, often with some of their colleagues. 'Spin-offs' of this kind account for the growing proliferation of small businesses in the media and creative sectors. In the absence of methods of direct managerial control, of the kind found in some traditional craft enterprises, there is little in the form of explicit control mechanisms which function to integrate work processes. Even methods of supervision whereby proprietors work alongside their staff may be inappropriate, since they offend 'professional' notions of personal autonomy and discretion. Further, the exercise of proprietorial control through the adoption of various charismatic, paternalistic, or autocratic management styles is of limited value. Highly-motivated employees are likely to feel patronised rather than motivated by such managerial appeals. What, then, integrates these organisations? Here is how the senior partner of one television company approaches the problem.

Management in a small independent television company

Everyone is treated equally. We have open production meetings where people are allowed to vent their anger and we have a regular Tuesday morning production meeting which is an open meeting for everyone in the company and that is chaired by myself. We do things like go through people's diaries and we go around each person and they will update us on what they are doing and also any problems they might be having. So it usually turns into an open debate about problems or suggestions on projects. For example, someone might say 'I'm going to America next week with a crew and I'm having problems getting visas – can anyone help me?' Or there might be problems about politics within the company, but usually those sorts of things are solved in private. If someone has a grumble about the way they've been treated, they usually come to one of us where they can do it in private.

Unlike most companies, we do encourage people to move forward, to convert their ideas into a programme and not come up with ideas and get someone else to do it, unless that's what they want to do. I mean you get some people who say 'I'm absolutely not interested in produc-ing/directing my own programmes. I'm very happy to come up with ideas, but for someone else to do it.' It's quite rare you get that – most people are closet programme makers, and if that's the case, then we try to encourage them to do that. Last year we made six programmes of that type.

What this business demands is lack of hierarchy. I don't go around and impose upon people my view of how things should be done; they come to me and say, 'I want to do it this way.' Providing it isn't a waste of money, I let them do it that way. We have a very long reputation of not over-spending on our programmes for our clients and that's due to the self-discipline of our staff, it's not due to me. What happens in this company is that the budget is an open system. The budget is available to anyone who wants to see it. I believe our system works. Everybody gets up in the morning wanting to succeed – it doesn't matter what they are doing, they want to succeed. You can make them fail by making them feel insecure, by making them feel as though they have no responsibility for what they do, by offering them poor working environments.

We don't have ogre shareholders round our necks – we're not owned by anybody else – it's our company, so we put the money back and we produce a decent working environment, then people feel they want to work for us. I mean, people are in here by 8.00 in the morning, the company is already up and running. The people are in here, enjoying themselves and feeling motivated to do it.

There is a profit-sharing scheme, but that's only if we can make the profits for sharing. We've only been going for eight years. We went into profit for the first time three years ago. Most of that was used to pay off various outstanding debts of one kind or another. This is the first year we can say we have made a profit which is a clear, genuine profit.

Management is a series of light and dark bits – it's not all light or all dark. It's not draconian, it's flexible. It's hues and shades, it's not all black and white. There are lots of subtleties involved and because there are people, each person brings their own spectrum of subtleties and it's very important that the company should use these subtleties to the best of its advantage. This company is a monument to people, to the way people like to do things and that's the way I want it to be. If it fails, it fails smiling. It's not going to be one of those dark, gloomy places where there is an absolute manager and nobody knows where the money goes. This company reflects the people within it, and that's what I want it to be like and that's what our clients like. When they come here, they are amazed at the enthusiasm of our people.

I walk around, I spend my entire time walking around, I know everyone by their first names. Leading by example is what it's all about. The army is often used as a derogatory system but if you take the US Army, which is on the platoon system or what is known as the 'buddy' system, everyone feels responsible for anyone else. The only hierarchy is that you know who will be the person in charge if there's a crisis. But up until that point, everybody's the same. If there is a crisis I will run ahead and deal with it, I will manage it.

Obviously I've got the executive producer role in the business. Most of what we produce here, whether it's for a corporate client or not, I will have to go and look at it. I am the most experienced programme maker in the company, I've been doing it now for twenty years. I have a good track record and I also write scripts and all the rest of it. People tend to get into difficulties on things through no fault of their own; it's either inexperience or they can't think of a way of doing it. So I spend a lot of time going around as executive producer. Now in order to do that I've got to be here and not stuck out of the way somewhere.

I still think I'm about twelve years old that's the trouble, and everybody else is to behave like a twelve-year-old. I think one of the great strengths children have is the ability to organise games and actually business is a game and children will do it by going into a corner huddled together, whispering, then coming out, telling the others what the rules are and then getting on with it. And I think that's the way that we do it.

Source: Interview with senior partner of a television company.

In creative, professional and high technology small businesses, the work process is broken down into 'projects', 'jobs', and 'accounts'. In this way, activities are organised according to client needs, for which particular individuals or groups within the enterprise will be responsible. Partners and employees organise their own and colleagues' work tasks according to the job requirements of their own projects, leading to an overall work process which, although highly fragmented, is dependent upon partners' relationships with clients (Meister, 1993).

There is little need for more direct forms of management control since work flows are constantly adapted according to client preferences. In this sense clients manage the work process and as such, there is little need for explicit management control. Just as the division between owners and employees is dissolved through the setting-up of these businesses as partnerships, any distinction between managerial and non-managerial functions is virtually non-existent. There are no managers and rarely are there partners with solely managerial responsibilities; it is unnecessary when the management of work is built into the professional–client relationship.

A further reason why the management function lacks specificity in these firms is because of the nature of their core competences. Creative, expert and professional employees obtain qualifications, training and work experiences that inculcate them with codes of practice and ethics which are designed to control standards and shape the nature of professional–client relations. As such, these function as modes of internalised control, rendering redundant the need for external managerial controls. Insofar as behaviour is regulated, it tends to be built into collegial relationships and expressed as professional ethics within 'training', 'induction', and 'shared experiences'. If there are explicit managerial controls these are applied to support staff such as secretaries, technicians, bookkeepers and other assistants. It is in handling these relationships that there are likely to be more work-place tensions, since hierarchical controls are contrary to the predominant culture of these enterprises. Attempts to exercise formal management over support staff may cause resentment because this contrasts vividly with the apparently ill-defined interpersonal relations between experts and professionals within the 'operating core'. Such divisions may be compensated by various office rituals; for example, the celebration of birthdays, office parties and after working hours drinks, when all employees are invited to socialise. Although embedded in personal networks, support staff are not partners and rarely have a stake in the wealth-creation potential of the business. Their jobs offer only limited opportunities for personal discretion and there are few other rewards in the form of personal recognition, challenge or self-fulfilment. They have few chances of promotion as they lack the professional qualifications and/or creative, technical or expert skills necessary to become members of the operating core. The absence of formalised management can also create job dissatisfaction since the work process is organised around specific projects, support staff are often subject to conflicting demands, yet are rarely trained to handle such interpersonal relations. For some, then, loosely-structured organisations may be a source of frustration and friction rather than job satisfaction.

If the cultures of traditional craft enterprises are strongly shaped by their proprietors, this is less likely to be found in professional and creative small businesses. The ethos of these reflects a strong 'individualism' and the professional desire for personal autonomy (Handy, 1990). As a result, business-based cultures tend to be less influential than the ethos of the profession. To compensate for this, proprietors and/or senior partners often give explicit attention to the development of business-based shared values. This may be achieved through appeals to 'customer service', the 'traditions' of the business, and 'pride in the product'. Such values are inculcated through induction programmes, socialising, and various in-house rituals and ceremonies which reinforce 'core' attitudes, beliefs and practices. But despite such attempts, the work process fundamentally orientates staff towards clients, an attitude which is reinforced by their identification with broader reference groups such as professional associations. As a result, professionals tend to view their employing organisation as a *resource* which can be used for delivering services to clients and for enhancing personal reputations. How, then, can commitment to the business be obtained?

Essentially, such enterprises are integrated on the basis of informal social networks and work teams. In staff recruitment, it is often difficult to assess in any precise manner a person's skills because of the indeterminate nature of creative, expert and professional tasks. Alongside references and job histories, knowledge of job applicants through networks of personal contacts is often considered important in the recruitment process. Since work activities are project-driven, as in television production or advertising campaigns, it is important that specialists are able to work together, pooling their talents and skills in a creative and productive manner. Hence, trust relations are important, and ever-forming and temporary work teams are the chief means whereby these can be nurtured. In these, work roles are often stretched beyond specific personal technical and creative competences and, hence, colleagues become interdependent upon each other for the success of their own goals. It is this interdependence of skills that is the key integrative mechanism which – because of their external client and professional orientations – might otherwise be excessively fragmented. These features are illustrated in the following description of working relations in an independent television production company.

Working relations in a small independent television production company

We don't put a lot of store in job titles but it doesn't mean to say that people haven't got a responsibility for certain things. But you can interfere in other people's things provided you recognise that it is their job to do it. At the end of the day, if a colleague says he's going to do something or won't do something, however much I like the idea, it's his decision.

We have business affairs meetings which is an attempt to bring slightly more communication into the place. If you're dealing with fifteen or sixteen projects at any one time it's very easy to get out of touch with what's happening. The important thing is that we do declare at every business affairs meeting, which happens every Tuesday at 9.30am, what is happening on a number of different projects so that anything which is started off – a new project – has to be described in terms of its aims and potential.

The formal meetings that happen are very few. There's internal departmental meetings which are specific to the skills of the people in those areas. There is a regular weekly development meeting just purely for those who are concerned with project development and for those who develop those projects so that they know what is happening. The business affairs meeting brings all the departments together to run through everything so that everyone in those departments knows what is happening. One person from each department, it doesn't have to be the head of the department, but he/she has the duty of passing this back to everyone else in their department. Then there's a whole-company meeting once every three months and we take whatever questions are hot at the time. But it's a small place and we're all in one building and it's all individually very close. There's not much status difference here. I think it's all fairly open.

Source: Interview with chief executive of a television production company

A key managerial issue for these enterprises is how to build teams and recruit colleagues who can fill appropriate team-member and leadership roles. Team leadership requires the exercise of delicate interpersonal skills because of the 'professional sensitivities' of colleagues. The ability to be both a team or project leader and a close working colleague is an essential component of successful organisational integration. Without this, individualism, division and segmentation can become pronounced as colleagues refuse to work together, withhold ideas, and 'role play', with the effect that the potential for creative synergy is lost. Clearly, project teams which consist of highly talented but often individualistic members may be reluctant to share and build upon each other's ideas. The importance of high-trust, harmonious team relationships and flexible working practices is revealed in our study of professional female entrepreneurs.

The need for flexibility, trust and work teams in creative and professional enterprises

These enterprises are characterized by the absence of rules and regulations, and of hierarchical relationships. Relations between employers and employees in such businesses can appropriately be described as 'egalitarian' or 'democratic' since all are expected to co-operate and do their utmost for the good of the common cause; namely, the attainment of the proprietor's objectives for the business. These features and the converse absence of formal, hierarchical and impersonal supervisory procedures are reflected in the following interviewees' remarks:

> We don't believe in a hierarchical structure but very much in a horizontal-type system . . . I believe very strongly that if somebody is very good at market research that we should invest in them as people and let them run their own sections. That's more or less what's happened so far. It's the best way to give people incentives. Our most recent acquisition is another market research company which is operated quite separately. People don't know about our ownerships at all. They're just autonomous . . . that's the way I see it developing along the lines of small service operations . . . People tend to work in little teams, so you might have a director and two or three executives who are responsible for a group of clients. They set themselves targets and they are responsible for keeping within them and making a

profit . . . So it's a small team approach . . . When we recruit, I look for personal qualities, their attitudes towards work. They have to be pretty informal and relaxed people with a sense of humour. We're not a rigid and inflexible organization. We have to know how much a person is going to work well with a small team.

My employees love their jobs because I involve them in everything. We have discussions about what we are going to do. I ask them what we should charge for the courses and why . . . and I say if you've got an idea, then draft it out. So we run it as a team. Therefore, once they come, they stay . . . I am certainly offering more than a male employer. I have to say this. I run it in a very personalized way. They come and say to me that they would like a day off and I say 'Right, fine, that's grand. Work it out between you.' I don't bother about it. They keep their checks . . . They know what they are paid per hour, they put down their total at the end of the week and one of the girls pays it out. It's only when they've run it for three or four months that I have a look at the figures . . . I certainly don't think a man would be so sympathetic or sensitive to the day-to-day domestic needs of these people. They don't have to explain anything to me . . . they don't have to tell me a rigmarole to justify their leave . . . But they are supervised on results. If I find a mistake I can blow my top. I can be extraordinarily patient when a person is learning and then I have a break point. I think they know where they stand. So supervision as such doesn't come into it. It's example and we talk about standards a lot . . . In hiring, aspects of their personalities are very high on the list. They've got to have a basic knowledge, but really they've got to work in a very small space and be able to get on with each other, because it's a team effort.

Somebody has described me as the company conscience. An awful lot of things don't even come to a management meeting let alone the Board because long before it ever gets to that stage they are saying that I won't have it. They know what I'll take and what I won't take . . . We had a manager a couple of years ago who came in with a management style which was based on the concept of checking up on people and she really would never have succeeded in our organization. She eventually resigned because I think she recognized it, too. The organization does, in fact, run on trust; on the assumption that people are doing their best and that their best is good. That penetrates right the way through . . . Every now and again somebody will take us for a ride but it's not very often. It's amazing what people can do and the energy and emotional hassle that you can save if you work on the assumption that it's a team . . . and we just work together.

Source: Goffee and Scase (1985, pp. 66–8)

ORGANISATIONAL ISSUES

The creation of effective work groups built upon the complementary competences and personalities of colleagues is the major management issue in many of these small businesses. This becomes even more significant when these enterprises expand. Because of the job expectations of creative, professional and highly-skilled employees, growth has to be pursued without the development of a specialist management function, without formalised rules and procedures and by avoiding the imposition of hierarchical control structures. However, processes of organisational growth often require the introduction of a management function which is positioned in order to support, rather than control, professional, technical and creative specialists. A challenging dynamic of business growth is to preserve professional autonomy while, at the same time, introducing legitimate managerial processes. Issues of growth, as they are confronted by both new and traditional entrepreneurial ventures, are the subject of the next chapter.

3

FROM SMALL TO LARGE
Handling entrepreneurial growth

Many discussions of business start-up give a strong emphasis to their growth potential (Birley and Westhead, 1990). Entrepreneurs are often regarded as those who offer the potential for job creation because of the employment which their businesses will generate. This view, however, ignores the personal motives associated with start-up as well as the complex management changes needed if small businesses are to grow. The motives for business start-up have already been discussed. It was emphasised how managers, scientists, professionals and other experts are attracted to entrepreneurship because of the independence which they hope to enjoy. For this reason they are unlikely to want to expand their businesses because this will lead to the need for structures, financial controls, and other formalised procedures associated with the employment of others. In order to avoid these, many entrepreneurs become specialists in start-up, setting up businesses which they then sell on when confronted with problems of growth. They prefer to be entrepreneurs rather than managers of human, financial and technical resources.

BARRIERS TO GROWTH

Among traditional craft employers there is a reluctance to move beyond the size at which it is possible to manage employees on a face-to-face basis by working alongside them within a process of mutual adjustment. In such working relations they can remain in control of staff by managing through example. To shift from this to a management style that requires the ability to trust staff in a hands-off manner so that systems of delegation can be established requires a fundamental change in proprietorial attitude and competence. Equally, the ability to manage according to rules, procedures and impersonal monitoring mechanisms requires entrepreneurs to develop management competences. This is particularly the case for those who have started their businesses on the basis of specific manual and technical craft skills. This can also apply to those who have managerial experience in large organisations since their skills are usually associated with specialist functional competences rather than more general, all-round abilities. It is such factors which are likely to hinder business growth, rather than lack of market opportunity or the inability to raise additional finance. At the same time, growth can disrupt interpersonal relations and create tensions that lead to the 'spin-off' of new businesses. Many of these problems are illustrated by the following extract, taken from a survey of small business owners.

The reasons why traditional craft enterprises fail to grow

It is usually necessary to employ additional staff if a small business is to expand. An employer will only recruit employees if he or she thinks it will contribute to growing profitability. Nevertheless, some business owners are prepared to forgo growth and the promise of extra profits precisely because it entails the employment of extra labour. In other words, attitudes towards the employment of workers will determine the extent to which the self-employed are prepared to relinquish their 'autonomy', small employers their direct involvement in the work process and within the larger enterprises, the types of organisational structure that owners will develop. But why do many business owners sacrifice the possibility of bigger profits through not hiring extra labour? Although the problem is sometimes financial in that it requires more capital, it is often mostly psychological. There seem to be two major anxieties which arise for many owners. First, the extent to which business growth limits their control over the activities of their enterprises. Secondly, how far they feel personally competent to cope with the organisation and supervision of labour.

These administrative problems were reiterated by an employer once with a labour force of more than seventy but now with fewer than six employees, who suggested:

The guys I've spoken to don't seem to think that they've got to keep books. This is where a lot come unstuck – they haven't got a clue. Just hard work doesn't make a successful business, you've got to have a good business mind. You've got to know how to negotiate, how to talk to people and how to do paper-work. So many fail because they just haven't got a clue of how to control or run a business.

Small employers are often against expansion because of the extent to which they would be no longer able to exercise their skills. The reluctance to become solely involved in 'administration' and 'paper-work' was reflected in the attitudes of an employer with two workers:

> I couldn't delegate work more than I do – certainly not by having more employees. Because I like being involved myself. I like to do the jobs myself. You've either got to have two men and work yourself or have eight men and not work yourself. In other words, just supervise them.

Small employers know that their relationships with their work-force have to change as the businesses grow but they are often very uneasy about it. There are fears that employees will lose respect once they become solely administrators and cease to work directly with their staff. A small employer described these tensions:

> There's only one way of managing direct employees in a small firm and that is to work with them. Never tell anybody to do anything that you cannot do yourself. You've got to be able to say 'Stand aside Jack and I'll bloody well show you'. That's the only way to get respect. My men know I can work as well as them but if they think they're carrying you they don't work half as hard. If they thought I was sitting at home on my backside five days a week they just wouldn't work.

If small firms are heavily dependent upon 'trust' for keeping overheads low and for operating effectiveness, it is clear that anxieties about its breakdown can be a reason why owners may choose not to expand. These doubts were expressed by one owner who, with a manager and a general foreman, personally supervised more than one hundred workers:

> Everybody says you've got to delegate but once you leave your hand off the button then your business will start sliding. The main thing is to be on top of it all the time, in touch with every section and really on the ball. If you get to the size where you have to delegate, you've got to work with the person involved so that his

mind works like yours and he's totally trustworthy. Personally, I
don't want to get to that size. I don't want to get to the point
where I don't know where the money's coming from and how
different jobs are going. I don't want to get to the stage where I
have to take somebody else's word for how the job is going.

The problems that arise with expansion were clearly expressed by
another owner with thirty employees:

I got to the stage where work wasn't being carried out satisfactorily. This came down mainly to supervision and the people I was
employing as supervisors and general foremen. I've got to say,
with regret, I didn't give enough thought when I picked out the
people for these jobs. I delegated to the wrong people and made
terrible mistakes. I didn't approach it in the correct way. I was not
strong enough with people, not firm enough. It's so difficult when
you start from the bottom and build up to the position I'm now in.
You've always done things personally and when you see it being
done by other people, you compare it to how you did it. I really
don't like being an office man. I used to run around in the van and
work outside and I still find it difficult not to become too involved.

Such were the supervisory difficulties that this particular owner had
recently appointed a general manager, who told us:

Up until last year the owner was really running the business on his
own and was attempting to control the whole thing by himself. It
just wasn't working – he was getting himself into a state. Maintaining control of labour by introducing 'in-between' management
was the major problem. He tended to try and economise on
supervisory staff, even on foremen and this aggravated the situation and didn't improve it. It was a question of getting over to him
the need for capable control in the field . . . It was just a
mushroom – a mushroom of chaos.

Source: Scase and Goffee (1987 a, pp. 55–61)

A major constraint limiting small business growth is the process of
mutual adjustment which characterises the work processes of small
businesses. The organisation of duties on this basis incorporates both
proprietors and their employees within an interdependent division of
tasks, out of which individual skills and competences become
defined. Although staff may be recruited according to their own

particular specialist skills, these do not constitute the *sole* basis upon which work tasks are performed. By working closely with others, individuals develop flexible and more broadly-defined skills which enhance the overall performance of the business. But business growth can destroy this process and therefore the motivation, morale and the competitive advantage committed staff give to an enterprise. Business expansion can lead to the restructuring of relationships, both between the employer and employees as well as among work colleagues. It is often necessary for proprietors to withdraw from their direct involvement in work processes and, instead of exercising managerial control through working alongside employees, to exercise authority in a much more hierarchical manner. A dimension of managerial control is introduced whereby there is a separation between managerial and operational activities. As proprietors become less involved in day-to-day operational matters, more of their time is devoted to negotiation with customers, suppliers, financial backers and other external agents. In this way, strategic and operational decision-making becomes separated from the execution of work tasks. If, at an earlier stage of the business, proprietors discuss business plans with their employees, this now becomes less evident, and with hierarchical control there can be the emergence of staff resentment as they perceive their employers to be 'non-productive'. This may threaten processes of mutual adjustment because employees become preoccupied with their own duties and thereby reduce the operational flexibility of the business as a whole. There can also be the deterioration of trust relations between employer and employees, and among work colleagues. As a result, forces emerge within the business whereby work procedures become more formalised according to rules, regulations, job descriptions, duties and responsibilities. This, in turn, reinforces the need for a separate management function with proprietors devoting more time to staff supervision or to their appointing managers, chargehands and others who can perform this task. Either way, there is generally an increase in management overheads, with ramifications for the competitive advantage of the business.

Because of these internal organisational forces, associated as they are with the dynamics of business growth, many proprietors choose not to expand. Growth requires such a fundamental shift in the nature of their businesses, and of their own managerial role within them, that many proprietors often feel unable to handle expansion. This is certainly the case with many manual craft owners who, for reasons of work experience and business background, do not possess the skills for setting up effective management systems. Equally, they are unlikely to possess the required competences for appointing staff who could take on managerial responsibilities required of a growing business. More usually, such skills are imposed in adversity by banks and other outside agents when firms encounter financial difficulties. The reluctance to introduce managerial skills into the business can lead proprietors to become 'overburdened' with strategic and operational matters, so that business controls become lax and the firm finds itself in financial difficulties. It is only then that proprietors recognise the need for expert input.

Hill Enterprises

Some nine years after the start of Hill Enterprises, as Robert Hill had often feared, his intricate financial dealings caught up with him. His considerably expanded enterprises were without adequate working capital and he was forced to bring in a new partner, Donald Robbins, who was willing to invest sufficient funds to keep the company going.

The immediate effect of the arrival of Robbins upon the operations of Hill Enterprises was negligible. Operations continued at the same hectic pace, and Mr Hill's personal activities did not appear to be appreciably different. He maintained his old 'office' and was still available to help out on any particular problems which arose. However, as time passed, it became more and more obvious to the employees that Robbins demanded a great deal of Mr Hill's time. Although he retained his desk in the corner of the shop for a while, Mr Hill soon set up new headquarters in the more plush surroundings of a new building that had been constructed adjacent to the shop facilities to house the sales and office activities of Hill Enterprises. Because of his new location and the demands made upon him by his new partner, Mr Hill was unable to spend as much time with the men in the shop as before. In addition, Robbins' apparent aloofness to the workings and problems of the production shop and its employees created resentment.

The employees noticed that shortly after Mr Hill had moved his office, the time-honoured method of 'blowing off steam' as a prelude to constructive effort on a problem became more and more ineffectual.

Mr Hill was no longer around to arbitrate really serious disagreements and his customary 'OK, now that we've got that out of our systems, let's get back to work', was absent. While blowing off steam was still an accepted practice, an element of bitterness seemed to be apparent in such outbursts that occurred. This bitterness, and a sense of resentment toward Robbins, permeated the atmosphere of the shop, with the result that many employees adopted a fatalistic attitude both toward the future of Hill Enterprises and their own personal future.

In this atmosphere a second major organisational change occurred. A new man, with the title of 'Works Manager', arrived to fill the vacuum created by Mr Hill's enforced attention to matters other than production. This man, Rod Bellows, was thirty-five years old, a Business School graduate, who had had ten years' experience with a large chemical company. He was hired by Hill Enterprises on the insistence of Donald Robbins, who felt that the production activities were inefficient and excessively costly. His appearance on the scene came as a surprise to the shop and production employees.

Bellows made the following comments about his responsibilities at Hill Enterprises shortly after his arrival:

This company has tremendous potential and an unlimited future. Robert Hill is a dynamic individual with great skills. He has certainly been successful to date. Mr Robbins and I will, I think, complement these skills and make the company even more successful. Mr Robins [sic] has the ability and experience to do some long-range planning and get our financial affairs in order, and I have the responsibility and ability to make our production activities more effective. A major part of the problem as I see it is that we use our time inefficiently in production. We don't have any effective scheduling procedures, or channels of responsibility and authority, with the result that the men spend a lot of time bickering with each other and conversing about things with which they should not really be concerned. Their job is to get out the production. Our job is to organise the production activities in such a way that this can be done at the least cost. The whole basis for the situation is that in the past Hill Enterprises has been small enough to be controlled effectively by one man. Now, however, we are no longer really a small firm and we cannot continue to operate like one. I have some ideas and some techniques which I plan to initiate which I think will increase the effectiveness and efficiency of our production operations by 50 per cent in very short order.

At the beginning of his third week as Works Manager, Bellows issued a series of changes in procedures to the production employees. Without exception these changes were made without consulting any of the men in the shop. All of them were issued in typewritten memos, a new practice which many of the employees felt was unnecessary and undesirable because of the effectiveness with which they felt the existing informal channels of communication had been used. The extent of the changes requested by Bellows was significant, ranging from changes in production scheduling techniques to changes in working conditions for individual employees. As the number of written memos coming from Bellows' office increased, the resentment towards them became more apparent, and a strong adverse reaction to his presence was evident on the part of the production employees.

Bellows also attempted to establish formal channels of communication within the production operations, for he felt that much needless discussion and confusion existed under the present system. He issued several organisation charts which described the 'approved' way in which communication was to be effected within the organisation. These charts were uniformly ignored by the employees, who continued to rely on the previously accepted informal channels of action. As time passed, the situation continued to deteriorate. Many of Bellows' acts and orders seemed to be in direct contradiction to Mr Hill's former policies and procedures. The individuals affected were confused as to which procedures to follow. Attempts to have Bellows clarify his orders either left the questioner more confused than before, or were greeted with a curt 'We don't have time to discuss that. It is perfectly clear. Just read the memo.' Within a few months many of the personnel talked of leaving to look for other employment, and a few did.

Nine months after Bellows had taken the position of Works Manager, approximately 25 per cent of the production force had taken new jobs. The morale among those remaining was poor and a significant increase in product rejects was experienced. But during the same period both Robbins and Bellows felt that important advances had been made in 'cleaning up' production activities and that the company was 'looking better all the time'.

Source: London Business School case study

The problems of growth associated with creative and professional small businesses can be even more complex and difficult to overcome. Again, these often arise from a lack of expert management competence but they can also be related to the job needs and work aspirations of employees. As discussed in the previous chapter, people with creative talents usually have little desire to exercise managerial control over others. They are more inclined to be interested in exercising their personal talents, to deliver professionally-determined quality services to their clients and to enjoy personal recognition. Accordingly, they regard their employers as providers of resources – financial, technical and human – which they can use for the purposes of achieving personal goals. There is likely to be little management depth in these businesses, and underdeveloped strategic capabilities because of the prevalence of 'professional' or scientific values. There are unlikely to be business plans; expansion is likely to be haphazard and customer-driven. Growth, as a result, is the outcome of a reactive response to market demand, rather than of *proactive* strategy. These problems can be summarised, taking the example of small, high-tech firms.

'Causes of crisis' in small high-tech firms

1 Weak general management.
2 Poor financial controls.
3 Product competition.
4 Diversification and acquisition.
5 Changing market demand.
6 High overhead structure.
7 Manufacturing and operating problems.
8 Cancellation or delay of major contract.
9 Poor marketing.
10 Price competition.

Source: Adapted from Slatter (1992, Table 8.1)

Of course, there are a variety of management functions to be undertaken within professional-based small businesses; tasks have to be supervised, co-ordinated and controlled. But this leads to the emergence of a management process without specialist management roles. In other words, professional and other highly-qualified staff undertake managerial tasks as part and parcel of their particular competences. Managerial identities remain latent to those of a more professional or technical kind and the only explicit management functions which they perform are undertaken in relation to support staff who provide administrative back-up. In the absence of coherent business plans and within organisational settings where there is little in the form of an explicit strategic apex, business growth can lead to operational inefficiencies and added costs. It is for these reasons that tensions emerge, as growth necessitates a specialist management function. This, in turn, can lead to the imposition of formalised procedures upon colleagues who attach considerable value to their personal working autonomy.

ROUTES FOR GROWTH

Those businesses which grow may do so in a variety of ways. Some do so by what may be described as 'confederate' structures. Such firms operate on the basis of a number of separate profit centres, each focused upon a particular service, geographical location or market sector. Colleagues are designated with responsibilities for each of these and when the point is reached at which the volume of trade requires the input of a specialist management function, a part of the growing business is hived off as a newly-created profit centre that again becomes the responsibility of a colleague. In this way, not only do these businesses reduce the need for a formalised full-time management function and associated overheads, but they also meet the personal autonomous work needs of colleagues. They are able to enjoy continuing self-development through new challenges, enhancing their specialist and technical competences without increasing excessively the burden of managerial and administrative responsibilities. In a sense, then, these businesses achieve growth without managers; the managerial function is incorporated within the day-to-day exercise of professional, technical and specialist skills.

Confederate structures

Confederate structures often have tensions associated with forces of centralisation and decentralisation. Although these may not be evident within each of the operating units – functioning as separate profit and loss centres – they can be apparent within the business as a whole. How and according to what procedures is performance of the separate units to be monitored? How much autonomy are they to have in the pursuit of their own growth strategies? To what extent are the separate strategies likely to weaken the synergy of the business as a whole? Decisions about these issues have to be taken, but by whom? In owner-managed businesses this is likely to be less of a problem, bearing in mind the legitimacy which the ownership function bestows upon proprietors' decision-making. But even so, there are severe constraints on the decision-making autonomy of owner-managers because of the quality of information that is available to them. Operational competences are located within the separate business units and information to proprietors is often 'filtered' by those who are responsible for these units and who are stakeholders in decision-making processes. As a result, proprietors are likely to rely excessively upon their own judgement and have insufficient consultation with their senior staff about strategic issues. There can, in other words, be problems of communication, information flows and decision-making within confederate structures.

In professional partnerships there are similar problems in strategy formulation. Decision-making for the business as a whole will often be subordinated to the interests of the separate operating units because each professional colleague's primary interest is directed towards the needs of their own particular clients. Overall strategy will be decided at infrequent meetings of those responsible for each of the profit centres. They may be concerned to protect their own vested interests, rather than to consider the overall interests of the business. Strategy formulation will be the outcome of bargaining between interested parties and there will be little in the form of a coherent 'core' which can integrate these into a long-term business plan. The outcome is for professional-based small businesses to be reactive to market demands, rather than to have explicit business strategies derived from detailed analyses of market forecasts and longer-term economic trends. Only after significant growth is it usually possible for such businesses to devote the resources necessary for strategic planning. If there is the nurturing of management skills associated with business growth, these are more likely to be in operational rather than strategic planning, derived from their own and their colleagues' technical capabilities.

51

The precise organisational characteristics of small-scale confederate structures are variable. Some are extremely loose-knit, with the operating units trading in a very autonomous manner. Others will be more tightly integrated through a variety of mechanisms. Sometimes these will be to do with the management or leadership styles of senior partners who may choose to 'arbitrarily' intervene in the decision-making processes of the separate operating units. In this way, the business is integrated by shared values expressed and embodied by the attitudes and behaviour of senior partners or owner-managers. This is particularly likely to be the case in those businesses in which there are founder-owners who are able to impose their opinions upon all aspects of their businesses, ranging from acceptable standards of performance, to preferences of personality 'types' in staff selection, to day-to-day working procedures. This is less likely in professional small businesses where highly-qualified staff are more inclined to shape the culture of their enterprises according to criteria of professionalism. Such businesses may grow through the generation of autonomous operating units, the control of which is more likely to be exercised through financial rather than managerial processes. Monitoring of performance will be undertaken mainly through standardised output measures – such as monthly management accounts – rather than according to forms of direct supervisory control.

It is not surprising that business growth, as reflected in various confederate structures, adopts a variety of legal forms. Within the long-established professions, the partnership remains the most common type of ownership. In the newer professions, such as the media, the creative arts, high technology and financial services, it is not uncommon for legal forms to range from franchises and licences to wholly-owned corporate subsidiaries. Franchising is becoming an attractive route for business growth, since the franchiser is able to exercise control solely through financial rather than managerial means. Equally, by pursuing growth through leasing and licence agreements, it is possible to increase market share without the day-to-day responsibilities of 'hands-on' management. Although with these arrangements the dice may seem to be loaded against franchisees and licencees, the latter do obtain some benefits. They enjoy market profile by trading under brand names that are well-established within particular niches. Many of the risks associated with start-up can be avoided because of the knowledge of 'parent' companies. By trading under licence or with franchise agreements, proprietors are able to benefit from the support of companies with financial and business expertise, but without being subject to tight operational controls.

Despite the tendency to achieve growth through decentralisation and fragmentation, some professional and high-tech small businesses are compelled to develop more clearly-defined management functions. The need to integrate the day-to-day activities of professional colleagues and to co-ordinate these within strategic business plans becomes more explicitly acknowledged. How, then, is growth to be managed so that professionals continue to feel in control and yet, at the same time, are prepared to accept the need for separate managerial mechanisms that will integrate and co-ordinate their different activities? This is a key issue, the resolution of which will shape the direction of business growth. Increasingly, it seems, those enterprises producing high value-added products and services take the view that growth through fragmented and confederate devolved structures is the more preferable option.

The Martin Parker Partnership

The Martin Parker Partnership started in the area of quantity surveying, but Cliff Martin's pursuit of growth led him to diversify into other professional services, focused around construction consultancy, in the early 1980s. He expanded his mainstream quantity surveying into project management work and then developed related specialist services such as building surveying, maintenance management, quality assurance services, design and construction consultancy.

Organisation design

At first Martin Parker adopted a classic partnership model of organisation. Partners contributed some equity to the firm on their appointment and then shared in the financial success of the partnership on a proportional basis. Additional salaried partners were also appointed who did not contribute to the equity of the organisation, but became senior salaried members of staff. Their expectation was subsequently to take an equity share in the business.

Both equity and salaried partners were expected to bring new clients with them when they joined and, once employed, to spend much of their time bidding for new work. This meant that the partners were extensively involved in meeting potential clients through their networks of contacts and dealing with existing clients. Frequently, they were away from the office. Even the salaried partners, who had more operational duties than the equity partners, would spend around 25 per cent of their time in generating new business and about a further 35 per cent liaising with clients.

Under the partnership the services operated independently, with a partner or associate (the level below a salaried partner) being responsible for an office (e.g. a branch office) or one or more project teams within each function. These teams typically comprised eight or nine people. Sometimes specialist groups would be set up to undertake feasibility studies into particular areas, using advice from the various teams as necessary.

In general the principle was that the partner who had first obtained the work continued to liaise with the client and to take any decisions pertinent to the contract throughout its duration. Although the partners functioned relatively autonomously, Cliff Martin kept track of all incoming and ongoing work through the monthly partnership meetings. As he also saw all the incoming post he was immediately aware if any problems arose and could contact the partner concerned at once to find out more about the situation, even if it involved one of the offices out of London. Martin saw this ability to keep tabs on work as crucial to ensuring that customer needs were properly looked after, although he tried to avoid interfering with the technical judgement or the business contacts of the partners.

Managing growth

One of the key moves in trying to manage growth was to introduce a managing partner in 1986. The managing partner was given, as his prime responsibility, the internal operation of the group. At the same time a number of support staff were brought in to set up and manage systems and departments spanning the whole company, including the financial operation, office management, marketing, information systems and personnel. Some of these appointments did not work wholly successfully, however, for a variety of reasons, many of which were to do with communications and relations with members of the professional staff.

The managing partner was appointed from among the senior partners. He had considerable experience in quantity surveying and great flair for bringing in new business, which led to his rapid advancement in the industry and a great deal of respect from other partners. After his appointment he naturally continued to spend a good deal of his time bringing in contracts for the partnership, but this inevitably involved him in long periods out of the office seeing clients.

Although the roles of the partners involved the marketing of the business, there was no dedicated marketing function. Following a long discussion among the partners in 1986 it was decided to establish an overall marketing plan. Consultancy assistance was obtained from a specialist firm which subsequently submitted a report detailing a co-ordinated marketing plan. Martin also appointed the Director General of the Institute of Marketing in an advisory position to offer marketing advice to the organisation.

Martin appointed his secretary as personnel manager in 1982. This role was largely an administrative one, in which personnel records were formalised and was part of the growing recognition of the need for standardised employment conditions and contracts. An administrative director/company secretary (an MBA) was brought in in 1986 to take charge of internal administration, accounting and the development of management information systems.

With the growth of the organisation, the administrative staff also began to implement standardised systems of management and control. For example, until 1986 the partners were responsible themselves for calculating fees and billing their clients. This meant there was no central control over debt collection or invoicing, with consequent problems for cash flow management. A chartered accountant was appointed as a salaried partner and given the title of financial director in 1987. His main task was to centralise cash management, although partners/directors retained responsibility for negotiating contracts and prices.

While the appointment of these support staff represented part of the move to a more co-ordinated and professional management, change could only be implemented slowly. The traditional standing of the partners was such that their authority remained intact, as was illustrated by a long discussion the directors had one day to clarify who could authorise a new desk – something that traditionally only a partner could do for one of his teams. Similarly, on a number of occasions, associates who were leading a project and liaising with clients had asked for clarification over the authority to sign letters. This apparently trivial issue was in fact an important one given that this carried contractual commitment in many cases and thus involved a partner's authority.

Finally, there was the continuing problem of supervision. Growth had been so dramatic that over the past couple of years several people had been promoted to team leader but had found it difficult to adjust to the sudden change from being one of the team. Frequently the comment 'I didn't think it was my job to do this' was made, as they tried to cope with their new managerial responsibilities.

Source: London Business School case study, prepared by Tim Morris, 1992

It is not only in 'high value-added' businesses that growth is managed through the development of decentralised structures. In those firms trading in more traditional sectors, the approach to growth through sustaining highly-centralised entrepreneurial forms is also under review. Chapter 1 provided a diagrammatic illustration of the typical low-skill entrepreneurial enterprise, in which owner-managers are located at the centre of the network of interpersonal relations constituting the structure of their business; they are at the heart of the communication and decision-making processes (see Figure 3.1). The legitimacy of their authority is derived from ownership, which gives them almost total discretion in terms of how they manage their businesses. Such enterprises may be described as strong power cultures (Handy, 1993), where employees have limited ability to challenge proprietorial judgement and decision-making.

Leadership style in the creative small firm

There is no one right way of managing small high-tech firms. There is an enormous range of leadership styles and many different ways of achieving the same results. However, the most successful firms (as judged by both sales and profit growth) appear to have a strong but democratic leadership style. Strong leaders with a clear vision and clear objectives are needed to manage the type of people attracted to working in small high-tech firms, but strong leadership does not work with high-tech employees if it is too autocratic. Well-educated staff find a highly autocratic style difficult to get along with and will leave, particularly in the

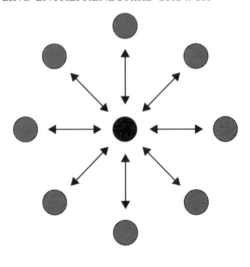

Owner-manager

Figure 3.1 A typical entrepreneurial structure

more people-intensive businesses. What is required is a democratic, or shared leadership style, where the chief executive allows plenty of opportunity for debate, but at the end of the day is prepared to take a decision even if it is unpopular among certain employees.

A style which relies solely on building consensus before a decision is made is likely to be too democratic. It would lead to slow decision making and be seen as weakness by subordinates. The chief executive must always be seen to be 'in charge', otherwise frustration and anxiety will build up . . . .The requirement for fast, analytical and bold decision making to deal with the extreme uncertainties in the high-tech environment means that one individual is unlikely to have the full range of capabilities necessary for high quality decision making. Chief executives of small high-tech firms need therefore to be supported by a team of functional executives with well-balanced skills.

Managers in the better performing firms work as a team rather than as individuals, although this does not imply the absence of friction among team members. The importance of working together as a team is stressed by many chief executives, including Compaq's Rod Canion, who uses a collective approach to decision making, recognizing that no one person on the management team has all the answers.

'We have a team process', says Canion, 'that leads to getting the best answer. We've encouraged all the things that it takes to have a team spirit. All companies want it, most of them talk about it, but few companies really have it, at least to the degree to which Compaq has been fortunate to develop and maintain it.'

The chief executive plays a key role in building team spirit by constantly being 'close' to employees at all levels in the organization. . . . Frequent interaction with managers and employees alike gives chief executives the real-time information they need to make fast decisions. Chief executives in the more successful firms prefer face-to-face communication and telephone calls to memos and reports, and have more regularly scheduled meetings with their subordinates.

Where decision making power is kept from senior executives by the chief executive, behind-the-scene politics may emerge and interfere with effective management. When this occurs, conflict between key executives arising from disagreements relating to organisational goals, key strategic decisions and interpersonal difference is likely to lead to secretiveness, the formation of coalitions and other unhealthy political behaviour. Some conflict within a top management team is healthy, and is probably inevitable in small high-tech firms where the top management are more likely to be well educated. However, conflict need not lead to negative political behaviour if the chief executive uses the right processes to encourage constructive debate and is prepared to outlaw behind-the-scenes politicking.

Being chief executive of a small high-tech firm is an extremely challenging job. It requires a unique blend of leadership and management skills to overcome the forces driving fragility. Few chief executives have all the attributes necessary to ensure success. It is therefore imperative that the chief executive is conscious of his or her weaknesses. This is particularly important where the chief executive is the founder of the company – although the founder may be a good entrepreneur, he or she often lacks people-management skills or specific business skills (e.g. financial knowledge). Founders of some of the more successful firms seem to recognize their weaknesses and take steps before any crisis develops to remedy the situation. This typically involves hiring (or appointing from within) a new chief executive while the founder remains, becomes chairman or 'retires' to head up the product development function.

Source: Slatter (1992, pp. 126–9)

For these reasons, proprietors may arbitrarily intervene in the tasks, duties and responsibilities of their staff, such that there is a lack of clarity in operational procedures. Accordingly, inefficiencies are likely to emerge with costs moving out of control, financial and performance measures becoming inoperative and cash-flow difficulties being more pronounced. In managing their businesses almost single-handedly and by inadequately developing the managerial competences of their staff, owner-managers become overloaded. It is often only at the insistence of 'outsiders', such as lenders, accountants or banks, that more formal and impersonal methods of management are implemented. The outcome may be reflected in the setting-up of functional structures according to which businesses are organised on the basis of a number of specialist spheres of responsibility (see Figure 3.2).

Although the imposition of such structures can ameliorate many of the weaknesses associated with entrepreneurial forms of organisation, new tensions can arise. As the Hill Enterprises example illustrates, staff can resent the imposition of procedures through which they are then compelled to communicate with managers and/or proprietors. As they perceive it, hierarchical and impersonal systems erect boundaries between the managerial and operational functions of the business. The imposition of rational monitoring mechanisms designed to measure output and productivity may, in fact, lead to demotivation. Cultures of 'informality' and 'indulgence' become superseded by those characterised by suspicion, resentment and

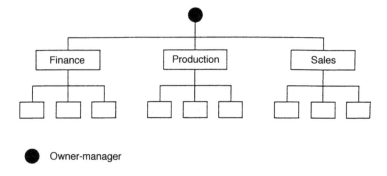

● Owner-manager

Figure 3.2 A functional structure

interpersonal friction. But even so, the setting-up of more formalised functional structures can fail to tackle the central issue facing these businesses: namely, the exercise of proprietorial authority. In practice, the imposition of functional structures can reinforce the highly centralised nature of these businesses, with owner-managers continuing to be overburdened with operational and strategic responsibilities and with managerial staff remaining underdeveloped. For these reasons, the breakthrough to long-term growth may only be achieved through the injection of strategic management skills and the 'prising-out' of founder-entrepreneurs.

Decentralised Structures

Systems of delegation can be set up so that authority and responsibilities are more diffuse within what become decentralised structures. This is often encouraged by the appointment of 'outsiders' who, with their more universal and transferable skills, are personally less dependent upon owner-managers and so are more likely to query their prerogatives. They are inclined to insist upon the implementation of effective systems of managerial delegation and, thereby, to wrestle control from proprietors. If skilfully handled, this can facilitate the emergence of greater management depth, allowing businesses to embark upon longer-term strategic growth. The tensions associated with these processes may be reflected in the establishment of 'quasi-organic' forms of organisation, according to which owner-managers attempt to both retain and delegate managerial responsibilities simultaneously. Their organisational strategy is to set up holding companies under which wholly-owned subsidiaries are established according to product lines and market segments. In this way, proprietors can extend both strategic and operational autonomy to the separate subsidiary units, but, at the same time, to retain overall control of the direction of the business as a whole. Management competences can be developed and market opportunities pursued from a number of distinct growth points simultaneously, and from the owner-managers' point of view, the performance of each subsidiary can be closely monitored.

Proprietorial control and managerial autonomy: the development of quasi-organic structures

There is much evidence to suggest that the proprietors of business enterprises are reluctant to delegate control to managerial staff and technical specialists. As long as their enterprises remain relatively small-scale, proprietors are, indeed, normally able to retain close personal control with minimum delegation. With business growth, however, there is a growing pressure to decentralise control if only because the sheer volume of decision making begins to exceed the personal capacities of proprietors. But as decision making volume alters, so too does quality; large size increases the importance of decisions and therefore discourages delegation. As a result, proprietors may attempt to maintain an extensive personal involvement in all aspects of decision making despite substantial business expansion. Edwards (1979) cites the classic example of Henry Ford, Sr., who, as late as the 1940s, 'refused to yield personal control over his firm, although the company had long since passed the point where it could be run as a one-boss workshop. Ford constantly interfered with engineering, production, and marketing decisions, but he even refused to permit his employees to maintain an organisational chart. Bankruptcy was narrowly averted only by the succession of Henry Ford II, who instituted modern management practices.'

Although this may be a rather extreme example, many proprietors are prepared to sacrifice economic returns for the retention of personal control. Indeed, evidence suggests that owner-managers and partnerships are less likely to add professional and administrative personnel, probably owing to their unwillingness to dilute their personal power. Although this might lead to less profitability, it maintains their existing organisation and stability.

The owner-directors that we interviewed tended to adhere to this pattern. It would seem from our evidence that their fears about delegation are related to four major factors. First, they are in control of family companies; they – often with other family members – own the substantial majority of the shares. Although the ownership and control of enterprises can be separated – with the latter delegated to senior managers – control is a resource which potentially can be used by managers against the owners. Thus, incompetent decision making and policy formulation by senior personnel can threaten a firm's existence and therefore deprive proprietors of ownership. Secondly, the markets within which such enterprises trade are, increasingly in the

1990s, characterised by considerable uncertainty such that 'formal' managerial structures are inappropriate. Indeed, during a period of economic recession they constitute expensive 'overheads'. To some extent, this explains the growing popularity within the personal services of various types of subcontracting arrangements which evade many managerial costs that might otherwise be incurred. Thirdly, there is a psychological resistance to delegation because owner-directors feel that many managerial tasks are unproductive. Finally, the rather haphazard process through which many of these companies have expanded and the owner-directors' lack of formal managerial training encourage the emergence of ill-defined, 'unbureaucratic' management systems.

There is, then, little evidence amongst the firms we studied of those 'mechanistic' forms sometimes described in management theory; on the contrary, there was a tendency for more 'organic' structures to emerge. According to Burns and Stalker (1961), 'mechanistic' management structures entail detailed job descriptions, clearly specified rules and procedures, and the co-ordination of work tasks through a hierarchical system of decision making. They are most effective where the work process can be readily subdivided into repetitive, routine tasks and the market situation is characterised by a relatively high degree of stability. 'Organic' structures, on the other hand, lack this precise specification of work tasks; procedures are broadly delineated, and there is 'the adjustment and continual redefinition of individual tasks through interaction with others' (Burns and Stalker, 1961). Management is less hierarchically arranged, and subordinates are vested with a considerable degree of autonomy and responsibility in the performance of their tasks. There also tends to be 'a lateral rather than a vertical direction of communication through the organisation, communication between people of different rank, also, resembling consultation rather than command; a content of communication which consists of information and advice rather than instructions and decisions' (Burns and Stalker, 1961).

The 'organic' form, then, tends to be more appropriate where flexibility and adaptability are required, fluctuating market conditions prevail, and specialist products are made in 'short runs'. It could be reasonably argued that, with deepening economic recession, these conditions are likely to spread to an increasing proportion of the British economy during the 1990s. Consequently, organic structures may be adopted within industries previously characterised by more bureaucratic systems.

In our study it is clear that proprietors deliberately develop what might be termed 'quasi-organic' management structures as a means of reinforcing rather than relinquishing personal control. As such, they are able to grant senior managers considerable autonomy within the context of a flexible and democratic organisational culture yet, at the same time, maintain proprietorial prerogatives. As we show below, this is not achieved without intraorganisational tension and conflict; nevertheless the strategy does allow owners to substantially retain firm central control despite the delegation of certain areas of decision making.

As Salaman (1977) points out, an organic organisational structure involves at least two elements: first, a loose definition of functions and tasks (a low level of formalisation); secondly, a 'spread' of authority among relatively autonomous managers able to exercise considerable individual discretion in the context of nonhierarchical work systems (a high level of decentralisation).

Salaman's case study confirms the view of several others that formalisation and centralisation can vary independently. He shows, for example, that the highly autocratic managing director of a medium-sized manufacturing company was able to mix a 'loose' organisational structure with 'tight' centralised control. Thus, although in the organisation studied jobs were not well-defined and lines of authority were unclear, managers were 'surprisingly lacking in autonomy and authority'. Indeed, the managing director's retention of 'final, and overwhelming, authority . . . was directly related to, and fed off, ambiguous and confused distribution and allocation of responsibilities and tasks'. The author concludes that, despite a 'friendly' atmosphere and 'egalitarian' culture, the actual distribution of organisational power remained tightly centralised.

There are close parallels between this study and our own, but whereas Salaman – justifiably in this case – rejects the term organic, we shall refer to 'quasi-organic' structures. This is because the proprietors in the present study combine, to some extent at least, informal and flexible work practices with a degree of decentralisation. Senior managers in these organisations are able to take some decisions some of the time. But the decisions that are delegated tend to be the less important ones and proprietors use a variety of techniques to ensure that managers 'independently' make the 'right' decisions. Furthermore, even formally delegated discretionary powers are subject to the direct and often arbitrary intervention of proprietors. This is a problem extensively documented elsewhere. Edwards, for example, notes the 'erratic and arbitrary' nature of entrepreneurial control within family firms in the

United States, which tends 'to undermine the exercise of routinised and formally organised power.'

In the absence of rigid procedures and hierarchical systems of decision making there is certainly greater scope for direct intervention by owner-directors. Thus, Handy (1993) suggests that the management structure of 'entrepreneurial organisations' can be thought of as a web, with the chief executive exercising considerable centralised control through intermittent but direct intervention. However, 'the web can break if it seeks to link too many activities; indeed the only way the web organisation can grow and remain a web is by spawning other organisations, other spiders.' ✗

Top management in these linked organisations, Handy points out, are normally granted maximum independence within centrally determined financial limits. This strategy is certainly evident among the enterprises we studied. Several owner-directors had created holding companies under which various subsidiary and associated enterprises were established. Ownership of the holding company is typically confined to owner-directors and their families, with some share participation extended to nonfamily directors within the subsidiaries. The directors of these subsidiaries are often given day to day control over their enterprises, but this is normally within parameters stipulated strictly by owner-directors.

Source: Goffee and Scase (1991, pp. 339–42)

ORGANISATIONAL ISSUES

There are many key management issues associated with small business growth. Even though there can be available market opportunities and ample sources of funding, proprietors often decide that the managerial risks are too high. As entrepreneurs, they deliberately decide to keep their businesses small so that it is unnecessary for them to develop the relevant management skills that business expansion inevitably entails. It is not unusual, however, for some proprietors to be 'forced' into pursuing growth strategies, primarily because of two major pressures. The first can be derived from the market place; in responding to customer demand, they can unintentionally find themselves managing ever-expanding businesses. The second may be as a response to demands from funding institutions, primarily the retail banks. Having funded loans and overdraft facilities at the start-up stage, they can be keen to encourage growth by giving further financial backing to profitable concerns. Finding themselves managing expanding businesses, with the concomitant management demands, many proprietors decide to review their business and personal life strategies. It is then that many of them choose to 'sell out' with the effect that their businesses become incorporated within larger companies. Others, however, overcome the barriers – using organisational strategies discussed in this chapter – to become the owners of very large businesses. Alongside this, others grow through acquisitions, mergers and takeovers. Big fish eat little, and it is this rather than indigenous organic growth which often accounts for the dynamics of business growth in the modern economy. It is to the managerial issues of these larger companies that we now turn.

4

MANUFACTURING
ORGANISATIONS

The twentieth century has been characterised by the growth of large-scale manufacturing corporations, producing goods for national and international markets. This has brought about a revolution in work practices, management, and organisational structures. As a result, there has emerged an organisational paradigm which has been seen to be appropriate not only for manufacturing but also for most other forms of organisation. The principles underlying this paradigm have been those of Fordism and Scientific Management. Because of the growth of mass markets, particularly in the United States, it became necessary for production to be organised on more rational, cost-effective criteria, compared with the systems normally found in owner-managed enterprises. In the latter, 'rule-of-thumb' management techniques determined methods of production which, in the high volume and competitive markets of the twentieth century, became inappropriate (Morgan, 1986). There was a wave of mergers and acquisitions in the 1920s which also raised fundamental questions about appropriate forms of organisation design. It was in response to these that the principles of scientific management became applied on a widespread basis for establishing rational organisational forms and procedures. Proponents of scientific management argued that all aspects of work could be analysed and then measured, so that the one best method could be determined. It was then the responsibility of managers to implement this one best way to bring about rational and cost-effective methods of production. 'Fordism' is the term most often used to describe these principles, since it was the Ford Motor Company which was popularly seen as the first organisation to systematically apply them to its operational procedures. As such, traditional craft-based forms of production were superseded by management techniques, work processes and technological systems which brought about the standardisation of work tasks and finished goods. Large numbers of craft workers were no longer required since under Fordist manufacturing systems they were replaced by semi-skilled operatives undertaking repetitive, routine tasks. This brought about nothing short of a revolution in the nature of work, because it led to the complete restructuring of management-worker relations, leading to highly cost-effective and efficient forms of administration and production – certainly by comparison with previous forms of organisation. It is only in recent decades that the assumptions of Scientific Management and Fordism have been reconsidered as an appropriate basis for the management of large-scale manufacturing organisations (Clegg, 1990).

THE FORDIST MODEL

The basic principles underlying any form of organisation – large or small, and irrespective of its products, markets and type of technologies – are those of integration and differentiation. Any organisational structure, allocating duties and responsibilities, is the outcome of decisions concerning how work processes should be broken down and integrated. Large-scale manufacturing organisations structured, as they have tended to be, upon the principles of Scientific Management reflect the extreme tendency to task fragmentation and differentiation, to the extent that there are often acute problems of work integration. This is reflected in all aspects of organisation, ranging from the specification of functional specialisms to the precise delineation of job roles. As a result, the boundaries between activities are sharply drawn so that there are significant structural, cultural and psychological barriers to organisational integration.

In manufacturing corporations there is often a sharp distinction between those functions associated with strategy formulation and those responsible for strategy implementation. This is reflected in hierarchical distinctions between senior, middle and junior managers. The formulation of strategy as a senior management activity may, as a result, be undertaken with insufficient consultation within the organisation as a whole. In effect, corporate strategies may fail to be fully implemented not because of their analytical weaknesses but because of the problems which result from excessive vertical and horizontal divisions. This may be because functional and departmental specialisms can also nurture introspective cultures which are focused upon their own vested interests and resource claims, to the detriment of cross-functional collaboration. Further, processes of strategy formulation can be impaired because departments hoard information in their desire to protect themselves from other functions. Equally, vertical sources of division can lead to the filtering of information flows, bottom-up and top-down. Executive corporate hierarchies can also create status orders, suspicion and low-trust relations between and among managers, an outcome of which can be excessive bureaucratism and resistance to change. Hierarchical and 'segmented' organisations, therefore, tend to foster management systems which are reactive rather than proactive to external changes, and consequently, to be inflexible in their operating procedures. If senior managers become excessively disengaged from day-to-day operational activities they may pursue misguided strategies on the basis of inadequate and 'filtered' information. Because of the divided nature of such organisations, they often have insufficient knowledge of key issues, as a result of limited access to the operating core and dependence upon informants whose objectivity in relation to strategic issues is questionable. The disadvantages of such organisations are perhaps best illustrated in their response to change; some observers suggest they nurture structures and processes which appear to deliberately stifle innovation.

Rules for stifling innovation

Rhetoric of change aside, the people in the middle at non-innovating companies generally do not see top executives acting as though they really wanted enterprise and innovation. There are notable exceptions; newcomers or those involved in a special R & D effort like a 'trial' can be very positive about the changes and change potential in their companies. But for most, the message behind the words of the top is that those below the top should stay out of the change game unless given a specific assignment to figure out how to implement a decision top management has already made.

In many instances, the behaviour of the top can be understood as though it were acting according to a set of 'rules for stifling initiative'. Imagine something like this hanging on an executive's wall in a segmentalist company, right next to the corporate philosophy:

1 Regard any new idea from below with suspicion – because it's new, and because it's from below.

2 Insist that people who need your approval to act first go through several other levels of management to get their signatures.

3 Ask departments or individuals to challenge and criticize each other's proposals. (That saves you the job of deciding; you just pick the survivor.)

4 Express your criticisms freely, and withhold your praise. (That keeps people on their toes.) Let them know they can be fired at any time.

5 Treat identification of problems as a sign of failure, to discourage people from letting you know when something in their area isn't working.

6 Control everything carefully. Make sure people count anything that can be counted, frequently.

7 Make decisions to reorganize or change policies in secret, and spring them on people unexpectedly. (That also keeps people on their toes.)

8 Make sure that requests for information are fully justified, and make sure that it is not given out to managers freely. (You don't want data to fall into the wrong hands.)

9 Assign to lower-level managers, in the name of delegation and participation, responsibility for figuring out how to cut back, lay off, move people around, or otherwise implement threatening decisions you have made. And get them to do it quickly.

10 And above all, never forget that you, the higher-ups, already know everything important about this business.

These 'rules' reflect pure segmentalism in action – a culture and an attitude that make it unattractive and difficult for people in the organization to take initiative to solve problems and develop innovative solutions. Segmentalism may not be the *only* problem of these companies with respect to change; there are also human failures, poor management, or absence of a real drive/need for change. But in general, segmentalism is the handicap. Segmentalist companies may not suffer from a lack of potential innovators so much as from failure to make the power available to those embryonic entrepreneurs that they can use to innovate.

Source: Kanter (1985, pp. 100–1)

Excessive organisational segmentation can also lead to the detachment of the strategic apex from the operating core in both functional and divisional organisational forms. In functional structures, which tend to be found in organisations trading with single or closely-related products and services, strategic decision-making can be concentrated almost entirely in the hands of the board and the chief executive. Departmental heads with their stakes in specific functional areas will tend to develop almost exclusively operational rather than strategic competences. Accordingly, such organisations can lack 'management depth' because of an absence of clearly-defined routes for management succession into strategic positions In divisionalised organisational forms, characteristic of corporations trading in a variety of product areas, strategic skills at the corporate level can be underdeveloped as divisional heads compete with each other for resources in the pursuit of their own sectional aims. Hence, there is often a tension between forces of centralisation and decentralisation, with those at the corporate centre bargaining with divisional heads about their respective areas of authority and responsibility. The latter frequently strive for greater strategic autonomy in the pursuit of their objectives, while those at the centre struggle to preserve their control. Such tensions often lead to ever-changing compromises, with corporate structures oscillating between periods of 'centralising', 'decentralising' and 're-centralising', depending upon the personalities, bargaining capacities and organisational resources available to the competing agents. Many large corporations have extended strategic responsibilities to their 'market-driven' operating units by transforming divisions into autonomous subsidiary companies, but subject to tight centralised corporate financial controls (Campbell and Gould, 1987). This overcomes the problems of information flow that mitigate against effective strategy formulation in functional structures and which may be even more pronounced in divisionalised forms of organisation when complex product ranges and market differences add to the complexities of corporate decision-making.

Of course, it is below the strategic apex of most large-scale manufacturing organisations that the principles of Fordism and of Scientific Management are likely to be most rigorously applied. It is within the processes of strategy implementation that there are the greatest pressures towards bureaucratisation, with the standardisation of work tasks and the adherence to rules and procedures. The key task of middle management is to convert strategic aims into operational work practices by setting performance targets, establishing quality objectives, and designing reward systems. In pursuing these aims the management process can become bureaucratised in ways similar to those occurring within the operating core. Indeed, the bureaucratisation of management, as described by Max Weber (1964), may be seen as an inherent feature of business growth. He discussed how the emergence of large-scale organisations requires the development of administrative systems whereby work processes are sub-divided into clearly-defined job tasks which are then integrated and co-ordinated according to hierarchically-arranged authority relations. Contemporary trends in organisational design often represent a reaction against formalised, bureaucratic systems of management (Peters, 1992). However, despite repeated attempts to 'broaden' the responsibilities of managers and to grant them greater working autonomy, there are significant countervailing forces reinforcing the bureaucratic constraints under which they operate. These include the application of information technology, which enables work processes to be subject to tighter forms of control and performance measures (McKersie and Walton, 1991).

As a result, managers find they are subject to two conflicting forces. On the one hand, their senior colleagues are challenging them to be more creative and enterprising in work contexts within which they are encouraged to exercise greater discretion and responsibility. On the other, the reality of managerial work – through organisational restructuring, the use of appraisal schemes, the implementation of new technologies and increasing competitive threats – is imposing greater demands and constraints within which managerial choices can be exercised (Stewart, 1991). It is hardly surprising that many managers are becoming disaffected with both the intrinsic and extrinsic rewards of their jobs and that they are exercising such options as early retirement, business start-up or simply distancing themselves, fulfilling their duties with a minimum degree of psychological commitment (Scase and Goffee, 1989). In view of these conflicting expectations, many corporate managers are experiencing stress and work-related anxieties and, more generally, they are subject to personal crises of identity, corporate 'solutions' to which may be offered in the form of management development programmes which may accomplish little more than raising delegates' morale and self-esteem.

Middle managers are responsible for exercising control over financial, technical and human resources, and it is through them that corporate strategic aims are implemented. They interface with both the strategic apex and the operating core and, together with their junior managerial colleagues, it is their responsibility to ensure that operational goals are accomplished. It is because of this that the characteristics of large-scale manufacturing corporations continue to largely embody the principles of scientific management. Despite recent trends to market fragmentation and product differentiation, it remains the case that most products can be manufactured most cost-effectively on the basis of standardisation. This constitutes their major feature and determines the nature of job tasks, the technology utilised and the worker skills required. Only in the past decade, with the adoption of 'flexible' forms of production, have the traditional principles of scientific management been challenged (Hammer and Champy, 1993).

This is particularly the case on the shop floor, where the application of the principles of Scientific Management and the development of mass-production technological processes have led to the extreme fragmentation of work tasks into job roles which offer few opportunities for personal discretion. The widespread use of assembly line technologies has led to work de-skilling, according to which operatives have little opportunity to exercise responsibilities; their tasks consist of little more than undertaking a very limited number of routine, repetitive activities. They are expected to behave as instruments of management, to be monitored and supervised by foremen, chargehands and front-line managers in order that production targets and quality standards are achieved. Within this process of task fragmentation, there is limited scope for group activity and social interaction, despite management's exaltations of team work, because assembly-line technology separates workers according to highly-fragmented job tasks. The advantages and disadvantages of work organised on the basis of the principles of Scientific Management can be summarised as follows.

The principles of Scientific Management

The key figure in the development of traditional approaches to designing work was Frederick Winslow Taylor (1865-1915; and nicknamed 'Speedy' in his lifetime). An engineer from Philadelphia, who trained as a machinist, Taylor was appalled by the inefficiency of the industrial practices he witnesses and set out to demonstrate how managers and workers could benefit by adopting a more 'scientific' approach. He felt that inefficiency was caused by what he called systematic soldiering, or the deliberate restriction of output by workers anxious to sustain their employment. Soldiering was easy because management control was weak, and because discretion over work methods was left to individual workers who wasted time and effort with inefficient working rules of thumb. Managers expected their employees either to have the appropriate skills for the work they were given, or to learn what to do from those around them. Notions of systematic job specifications, clearly established responsibilities, and training needs analysis were not appreciated. Taylor sought to change that.

Taylor argued that manual and mental work should be separated. Management, he claimed, should specialize in planning and organizing work, and workers should specialize in actually doing it. Taylor regarded this as a way of ensuring industrial harmony, as everyone would know clearly what was expected of them and what their responsibilities were. He also saw the clear advantages in making individuals specialize in activities in which they would become expert and highly proficient.

His technique for designing manual jobs involved the following steps. First, decide the optimum degree of task fragmentation, breaking down complex jobs into their simple component parts. Second, determine the most efficient way of performing each part of the work. Studies are carried out to discover the one best way of doing each of the fragmented tasks, and to design the layout of the workplace and tools to be used so that unnecessary movements are eliminated. Finally, select and train employees to carry out the fragmented tasks in exactly the one best way, and reward them for above average performance.

Clearly, task fragmentation can have a number of advantages for the organization that applies it. Individual workers do not need to be given expensive and time consuming training, and those who leave or prove to be unreliable can easily be replaced. Specialization in one small task makes people very fast at it. Less skilled work is lower paid work. And it is easier to observe and control workers doing simple activities.

But task fragmentation also has disadvantages for those subjected to it. The work is repetitive and boring. The contribution of the individual to the work of the organization as a whole is comparatively meaningless. Monotony can lead to apathy, dissatisfaction and carelessness. The individual develops no special skill or knowledge that might lead to promotion or to better work in another organization. One of the main criticisms of Taylor's work is that it lacked any sustained attention to human needs other than those concerning money and rest. His approach to job design appeared to create efficient ways of working, but created fragmented and dissatisfying jobs that were unlikely to develop employee skills, commitment and high performance in the long run. Subsequent research has suggested that the expression of human needs at work is richer and more complex than Taylor's methods assumed.

It is often argued that many people prefer the simplified types of work that Taylor's approach produces. This argument cannot be generally accepted for two main reasons. First, there are probably not enough people available with the high level of tolerance of boredom required to carry out simple and meaningless tasks efficiently. Most people have higher levels of ability and higher expectations of working life. Second, they have a physiological need for sensory stimulation, for changes in the patterns of information that feed to the senses to sustain arousal. When we do not receive that stimulation, our sensory equipment 'switches off'. There are several ways in which poor psychological well-being affects performance through the costs of absenteeism, labour turnover, careless accidents and wilful sabotage.

Why has Taylorism retained its popularity? There are three reasons.

First, it is a plausible, easy and cheap set of techniques which appear to work. Managers (particularly in Britain) often prefer common sense, practical ideas to more complex and sophisticated techniques, especially those based on 'social science', an enterprise which is still widely regarded with suspicion and scepticism. Task specialization reduces work in progress and throughput times, takes less space, and simplifies production control. These clear, 'hard', short-term gains may outweigh the less certain and less quantifiable longer term costs and disadvantages, which rest on 'soft' arguments about the nature of human reactions to work. It is always easier to blame workers who have the wrong skills, wrong attitudes and wrong values, than to blame a systematically prepared job specification.

A second less obvious, and to managers less acceptable, explanation is that Taylor's approach to work design perpetuates the higher status and authority of managers, who work in clean offices, do no manual work, take all the responsibility and the decisions, and go home with higher financial and symbolic rewards. Groups of office and shop floor workers who have discretion over the performance of meaningful sections of an organization's operations are a greater threat to managerial legitimacy than individual workers who have little or no idea how their fragmented tasks contribute to the work of the organization as a whole.

A third reason is the lack of credible alternatives. Many managers are aware of the problems of scientific management and are looking for 'a better way'. But accounts in the popular management literature are often too insubstantial to serve as examples for other organizations, and reports in the academic domain are often expressed in a language that obscures their wider application, and damages their credibility.

It is therefore wrong to dismiss scientific management methods as disused and dated. Some organizations have departed from that approach and adopted other approaches. But Taylor's ideas have become a central feature of the taken-for-granted organizational recipe that many managers apply to the design and redesign of work, without serious question or challenge.

Source: Buchanan and McCalman (1989, pp. 10–13)

One of the most fruitful analyses of work experiences as shaped by a variety of technological, organisational and management processes in manufacturing is Blauner's *Alienation and Freedom* (1964). This discusses how the contrasting work settings of the chemical, textile, printing and automobile industries have different outcomes for shop-floor workers' feelings of job satisfaction. In Blauner's view, automobile workers obtain little satisfaction from their jobs because, by comparison with others, they experience the greatest feelings of powerlessness, meaninglessness, isolation, and self-estrangement. Automobile workers, as an example of those working in large-scale assembly-line technological processes, experience powerlessness because they are unable to exercise control over both the quantity and quality of their work. In other words, the 'intelligence' and 'skill' required of craft workers are built into the technological processes which then dictate to operatives how and when, and according to what specifications, work tasks are to be performed. Workers are little more than appendages to machines, closely monitored by management. Their work is also meaningless, since through the application of Scientific Management, tasks are fragmented, standardised and routinised. Problem-solving and decision-making are taken from operatives and become the responsibility of front-line and middle managers. As a result, shop-floor employees obtain little sense of purpose from their work. This is reinforced by feelings of isolation, because they are physically separated from each other through a technologically-determined division of labour. Work is regarded solely as a source of income, with operatives being self-estranged because their jobs inhibit the exercise of creativity and personal development. Instead of being a source of self-enrichment, employment becomes defined as an instrumental activity which simply enables employees to meet their 'basic' social and economic needs of survival. In sum, twentieth century manufacturing methods generate alienation, and with it a variety of economic, sociological and psychological consequences.

Some consequences of mass-production technology

Two consequences of assembly-line technology and work organization, the 'massified' occupational distribution and extremely large factories, are the critical elements underlying the social structure of the automobile industry. The mass of workers are at a uniform level of low skill, and the majority of men in assembly plants are paid almost exactly the same rate. The relative lack of occupational differentiation by skill, status, or responsibility creates an industrial 'mass society' in which there are almost no realistic possibilities of advancement. The industry therefore lacks a built-in reward system for reaffirming its norms and integrating the worker into a community based on loyalty to the company. Social alienation is further intensified because automobile workers are low skilled, without strong occupational identity, and loyalty to an independent craft is not possible for most employees.

In addition, the technology and elaborate division of labor require a large physical plant and a sizable work force. As a rule, the larger the factory, the more tenuous is the employee's sense of identification with the enterprise and the greater the social and sympathetic distance between him and management. The automobile assembly plant stands at the apex of the historical development toward larger and larger factories . . . .Automobile production may be the ideal example of an industry where large plants and firms have most contributed to the extreme development of an impersonal work atmosphere and to the breakdown of sympathetic communication and identification between employees and management.

In these circumstances, social control rests less on consensus and more on the power of management to enforce compliance to the rule system of the factory, a power sometimes effectively countervailed by the strong labor union, which has a legitimate mandate to protect certain interests of the workers. The compelling rhythms of the conveyer-belt technology and the worker's instrumental concern for his weekly pay check are more important to him than internalized standards of quality performance or an identification with organizational goals in providing the discipline that gets work done in an orderly fashion. The social personality of the auto worker, a product of metropolitan residence and exposure to large, impersonal bureaucracies, is expressed in a characteristic attitude of cynicism toward authority and institutional systems, and a volatility revealed in aggressive responses to infringements on personal rights and occasional militant collective action. *Lacking meaningful work and occupational function, the automobile worker's dignity lies in his peculiarly individualistic freedom from organisational commitments.*

Source: Blauner (1964, p. 177)

Of the many outcomes of work alienation, those that have attracted the most attention are concerned with how production methods foster the pre-conditions for industrial conflict, high labour turn-over (in some labour market conditions), absenteeism and the manufacture of inferior quality products. But of the many weaknesses of Fordist methods of production, the relative inability to adapt to changing market needs is probably one of the more striking features. The heavy investment required for setting up large-scale production processes locks capital into the production of goods for specific markets. Assembly-line technology is largely incapable of producing anything other than standardised products, and if there are changes in market demand, the re-tooling associated with adapting and developing new products is often expensive to implement.

At the same time, the bureaucratic character of management systems, based upon the division of specialist functions, makes decision-making slow and cumbersome. Further, a basic principle of Scientific Management, with its emphasis upon the separation of the functions of conception (that is planning, decision-making and control) from those of execution (the actual performance of work tasks on the shop floor) creates a sharp division between 'managers' and 'workers' (Braverman, 1974). Such forms of organisation can generate low-trust relations, with both groups suspicious of each other's objectives. These circumstances are unlikely to foster cultures conducive to innovation and change; indeed, Fordist methods of managerial control may inhibit creativity among those responsible for research and development Even the alleged strengths of Fordism – that it can take advantage of the economies of scale – can be challenged. Fluctuations in market demand may result in excess production capacity and unnecessarily high overhead costs which have to be financed from less than optimum levels of production. But perhaps most importantly, because of the 'human' problems generated – absenteeism, industrial disputes, labour turnover, low job satisfaction – the economies and cost savings associated with assembly-line technological processes and large-scale forms of organisation are often not fully realised.

THE POST-FORDIST MODEL

The above reasons help to explain contemporary attempts to abandon the more extreme forms of Fordism and to replace it with operating practices which are more likely to encourage product innovation and employee commitment for more effective competition. There are several market-driven factors which are compelling organisations to review their traditional methods of production. Among the more important of these are growing customer resistance to poor quality products and increasing needs for 'specialist' goods and services which create niche markets that, in turn, require more flexible production processes and distribution systems. Alongside these external forces, there are various internal practices compelling large-scale corporations to abandon their traditional methods of management and production. There are suggestions that many employees expect to enjoy a greater degree of working autonomy, according to which they can enjoy a higher level of job satisfaction. As a result senior managers may redesign jobs and restructure organisations so that job needs for greater self-fulfilment are more adequately met.

Although this is the *overall* direction of contemporary organisational change, established Fordist methods of production continue to predominate, even though the more rigid features may have been modified. Many companies find it difficult to restructure because of the high costs associated with abolishing traditional methods of assembly-line technology. Further, the cultures of many companies sustain ideals of these traditional methods; they are still perceived to embody the most rational and cost-effective organisational principles. Equally, the training and competences of managers and supervisors encourage them to sustain the operating practices of Fordism. They have acquired specialist functional skills which are only relevant within bureaucratically co-ordinated divisions of labour. If these are abandoned, the organisational settings which sustain their skills are also eliminated, making their own competences redundant (Kanter, 1989). Further, the principles of Scientific Management create hierarchies of responsibilities which, in turn, are reflected in status orders and salary gradings, encouraging many managers to resist change. Such barriers to change are endemic within a number of organisational processes.

The New Organisation?

Management gurus are constantly telling us that business organisations are in the process of radical change. They talk about flat structures, the absence of hierarchy, decentralisation and devolution of responsibilities. They see the end of secure careers for corporate managers. Most of these predictions are speculative, rarely drawing upon hard evidence. Most examples are from American high-technology corporations – such as IBM, Hewlett-Packard and 3M. Management thinkers act as though such models are directly transferable to all industrial countries and to all types of corporations, regardless of product or skill levels. But it is not clear whether the model fits the majority of UK companies, located in manufacturing, retailing and 'low-skill' service sectors. There are many barriers to the adoption of this New Organisation in the UK. It pre-supposes 'high-trust' cultures, where employees are trusted by their managers and are left alone to get on with their jobs. But Britain is a low-trust society. The legacy of the poor industrial relations of the 1970s and the notorious British class structure nurture suspicion and division. This is reflected in many large organisations in relations between managers as well as between management and workers.

The New Organisation requires new abilities among managers. Instead of managing through rules and formal procedures within hierarchies, sophisticated interpersonal skills are needed. The New Organisation demands leadership through inspiration, motivation and commitment rather than management by memos from behind closed doors; teamwork and co-operation rather than competitive individualism; and general talents in negotiation, goal setting and human resource management. But the training of managers in Britain emphasises the need for specialist technical skills to the neglect of 'intangible' and 'soft' human resource skills. If it is to function efficiently, the New Organisation needs adaptable employees who are prepared to cover for each other within teams and operate with broadly defined job roles. But in Britain, the system educates future employees to expect security, routine and stability in their job tasks. The educational system does not stimulate creativity and the search for excitement, change and challenge at work. But the New Organisation needs such forces. This leads to a further obstacle. Managers in Britain are ill-trained to handle programmes of change and corporate restructuring. The aims and objectives of change programmes are usually clearly defined. But these objectives are often only partially achieved because of inadequacies in the management and implementation of the change process. The New Organisation abolishes long-term careers, security and status. But these are central to the British economic culture and are important sources of motivation. The ideals of the civil service and the traditional professions continue to shape business culture despite a 10-year flirtation with entrepreneurship and risk-taking. An essential ingredient of the New Organisation is a culture which emphasises innovation and change. To bring this about, corporate leaders need sophisticated techniques and skills. A change in corporate culture demands long-term strategies, whereas British organisations tend to pursue counter-productive 'quick fixes'.

Does all this mean that strategies for developing the New Organisation are doomed? The problems can be overcome – as witnessed by the successes of organisations such as the TSB, parts of the Reed International group and Mercury Communications. There is now sufficient data available to guide managers in their pursuit of the New Organisation. Corporate leaders, following the Japanese example, should change their personnel policy. This is the starting point for creating cost-effective, competitive, proactive New Organisations. The New Organisation already flourishes in some sectors of the economy – in advertising, publishing, television and film production, and in parts of financial and professional services. The challenge facing British management is to apply these patterns to large public- and private-sector organisations. It is in these corporations that there are the greatest obstacles to developing new management styles. But in view of the broader culture of British society, perhaps the creation of innovative bureaucracies in large areas of these sectors is as far as the process is likely to go.

Source: Scase (1991)

Those organisations which are attempting to change are sometimes described as 'post-Fordist' in order to emphasise the extent to which they are adopting organisational paradigms that are in sharp contrast to those prevailing until the 1970s. Although they can be highly diverse in their structural and cultural features, they have a number of core characteristics which are being adopted by many large manufacturing corporations in the United States and Europe (Peters and Austin, 1986). One of the most significant organisational shifts is towards increasing decentralisation of production. Under the umbrella of the strategic apex, there is a general move to break up the operating core into a number of semi-autonomous operating units. Depending upon the nature of products, markets and technological imperatives, the aim is to abandon bureaucracy, to flatten management structures and to empower employees at the point of production. Product and market divisions are often reconstituted as subsidiary companies, with managers replaced by those who are expected to act as corporate entrepreneurs, taking on both strategic and operational responsibilities. Managers, as 'leaders', are expected to develop human resource strategies whereby their staff will be flexible in their working patterns, prepared to undertake broadly-defined job roles and to be sufficiently motivated so that responsibilities can be delegated to them (Wickens, 1987). This is in sharp contrast to Fordist methods of production in which managerial responsibilities are highly centralised with performance monitored by layers of supervisors, chargehands and others. One of the competitive strengths of post-Fordist organisations is that they are more cost-effective since they require fewer managers and have lower management overheads. This can only be achieved if staff are committed to their employing organisations, since, without this, responsibilities cannot be delegated. The shift from traditional types of organisation to more 'flexible' or 'adaptive' forms, as this affects characteristics of the operating core, may be described as follows.

Paradigm shifts in management

From: $\longrightarrow$	*To:*
• *Fordist*	• *Post-Fordist*
• Precisely-defined job roles	• Broadly-defined job roles
• Specialist skills	• Transferable skills
• Tight control	• Loose control
• Bounded responsibilities	• Autonomy and discretion
• Rules and procedures	• Guidelines for behaviour
• Closed communication	• Open/fluid communication
• High status differences	• Low status differences
• Low-trust relationships	• High-trust relationships
• Prevailing custom and practice	• Innovation and change
• Colleagues as individuals	• Colleagues as team members
• Invisible management	• Visible leadership

A case study illustration of the required changes in organisational practices is described below.

Organisational change at SP Tyres

John Mullen is proud of the 12 neatly drawn charts which festoon the wall in the textiles area he is in charge of at SP Tyres factory at the old Fort Dunlop site near Birmingham. With neat lines the charts track the progress made by the small cell of workers he leads in improving quality and productivity. The latest addition records how the cell has introduced a just-in-time system to reduce stock levels and work in progress. Where there once would have been 120 rolls of textiles in stock awaiting processing there are just 11. Mullen, who was recruited as a manual worker, talks confidently to Ian Sloss, the company's manufacturing director, about the cell's performance, emblazoned on the graphs. Their conversation is symptomatic of the way SP Tyres has transformed the once ailing factory. The skills Mullen has learnt to lead the cell, such as statistical process control and quality management, have come from an extensive training programme. His position as cell leader is testimony to the company's drive towards a less hierarchical management structure which gives more responsibility to a better trained shop floor. The ease of his conversation with Sloss is an indication of the way the company's vastly improved employee involvement and communications programme has cut across traditional demarcation lines between workers and managers. For there seems little doubt that SP Tyres has become a roaring success since the Japanese Sumitomo Rubber Industries took over the site after its acquisition in 1985 of Dunlop's European tyre operations. SRI did not have the advantages of many other Japanese inward investors in the UK. Most of the buildings on the site date back to 1916. It could not select carefully vetted workers. Far from having a single union/no-strike agreement the company had to deal with a clutch of craft and general unions. Yet production at SP Tyres is 50 per cent up on that of 1984, with a third fewer workers. Waste and warranty costs as a percentage of turnover have been more than halved. The company's market share in all product sectors has increased. An annual loss of £20m was transformed into a post-tax profit of £3.7m in 1988. SP Tyres, which also has a factory in Washington, Tyne and Wear, and a retreading plant near Manchester, is well placed to benefit from recent major investment plans announced by Japanese car manufacturers Nissan, Honda and Toyota, seeking to establish a European base for the 1990s.

If the success is obvious, the causes are far more difficult to pin down. Why have British managers and workers been so much more successful under SRI's ownership than under the previous British regime? According to Sloss the place was a shambles when he arrived at Fort Dunlop after Dunlop closed its factory at Speke on Merseyside. He says: "It was run by unions on the one hand and bureaucratic accountants from London on the other, who thought managing was ringing up to tell us how many tyres to produce." There was a hierarchy of seven canteens. The manual workers' canteen had one of the most popular bars in the neighbourhood. By the early 1980s the company was heading for bankruptcy. The takeover itself had an effect on employee attitudes and performance. SRI was able to take harsh decisions over redundancies which the incumbent management felt unable to face. Every worker retained knew that this was the factory's last chance. Yet the involvement of a Japanese company intent on making the plant a success also provided a sense of security after the years of cut-backs and insecurity about threatened closures. SRI has invested about £10m a year in the site. Little of the improvement is attributable to the sweeping introduction of new technology, though. Some of the productivity gains are due to redundancies which cut the workforce from 8,500 in the early 1980s to about 2,500 last year. But many of the changes have been much more qualitative. The most important was adopting a new approach to communication as the basis for management authority and credibility.

The details of the SP Tyres communication programme are fairly unremarkable. There is a monthly team briefing, with information spreading down from the board room to the shop floor. Three times a year board members meet groups of shop floor workers for question and answer sessions. The company has set up multi-disciplinary teams to tackle production problems. What matters is how this dovetails with the company's approach to management. Information can flow freely only if barriers are removed. Effective communication demanded that the status symbols of the old Dunlop days – such as separate car parks – were removed. Changes were introduced; everyone now wears the same uniform. As Gerry Radford, the company's chairman, explained in a recent presentation to the Japanese Chamber of Commerce: "This is not some eccentric part of Japanese culture, imposed from SRI's headquarters in Kobe. It genuinely makes everybody feel part of the same team and more at ease with each other in communicating ideas. Communication is not merely through the spoken or written word, but through our whole style of behaviour." Sloss stresses the importance of continual informal discussion, which is borne out by the relaxed way he chats on first name terms with workers in the plant. Yet he believes communication can be improved. "The formal briefing meetings do not give people much room to voice their opinions. We need to develop more two-way communications." The apparent informality belies SP Tyres' determination. Its approach to training is a clear example. The company's extensive quality training programme started in 1986 with about 1,000 staff being trained in statistical process control. It has since been extended to involve all staff, from sales and marketing to accounts, in a total quality programme. Sloss explains: "After the initial programme we realised about 85 per cent of our quality problems were not on the shop floor." Yet contrary to the conventional wisdom that companies need to take a more systematic approach to spending on training, there is no training budget and Radford admits he has no idea how much is spent on training. This is because most of it is done relatively inexpensively in-house by multi-disciplinary teams, led by senior managers. These teams take responsibility for training other members of staff, often in areas outside their occupational expertise. A production engineer might find himself training others in quality concepts. With its new management style based on communications as the foundation, the company is moving on. An aborted attempt in the first years after the takeover to introduce quality circles will be resurrected; there is widespread confidence that it will be a success. Just-in-time production will gradually spread through the cells in the factory, as will more new technology. Sloss says: "You can only do these things when attitudes are right. Now we can really make best use of just-in-time and new technology to improve quality and increase output."

Source: Leadbetter (1990)

Through post-Fordist work practices, it is possible for manufacturing organisations to be innovative and to concentrate upon short runs of production geared to the fluctuating needs of specific market niches. Flexible working practices and the redesign of jobs into broadly-defined work roles make this possible, but only if the appropriate technology is available. Developments in new technology – robotisation and computer-based information systems – enable manufacturing companies to produce short runs on a cost-effective basis. Equally, innovations in information technology and telecommunications enable companies to develop post-Fordist forms of organisation, since instead of strategic and operational functions being undertaken by specialist functions, those at the strategic apex are able to monitor the day-to-day performance of each of the separate operating units. The application of information technology is reducing the need for middle managers, as it becomes possible for organisations to be simultaneously both centralised and decentralised (Häkansson, 1989). Those responsible for the separate operating units are encouraged to be innovative and risk-taking, but they are tightly constrained by the monitoring of management information systems. In many ways, post-Fordist manufacturing companies consist of constellations of semi-autonomous operating and/or strategic business units, but the separation of power and responsibilities as these are concentrated within the strategic apex and devolved to the

86

separate units can be ambiguous, fluctuating
source of organisational tension.

The 'confederate' character of these organisat
the fact that many of them have 'slimmed d₀
cores in order to concentrate upon the produc
limited range of products by relying heavily up
out-sourcing for key aspects of their production p....
past manufacturing enterprises tended to have integrated work flows
with final products assembled in house, new organisations often
consist of networks of production units arranged on the basis of a
spatial or territorial division of labour (Sabel, 1982). Such networks
may consist of a number of wholly-owned subsidiaries, but these
can also be independent subcontractors and out-sourcers who,
despite their legal standing, will be dependent upon such inter-
organisational networks for their survival. These forms of organisation are developing not only in manufacturing activities but also in
relation to other corporate functions. In high-technology companies
the large capital outlays associated with research and development are
forcing companies into strategic alliances of various kinds so that
they can pool the costs of research and development but retain their
production and marketing autonomy (Lorange and Roos, 1993).

Strategic alliances in Europe

Last week, Philips, the Dutch electronics group, and Grundig, the
German consumer electronics company in which it owns a 32 per
cent stake, said they would join their video and cordless telephone
operations. On the same day, Olivetti, the Italian computers and office
equipment group, announced an alliance with Canon, the Japanese
camera and electronics group, to produce bubble inkjet printers. These
moves are part of a growing trend among Europe's ailing electronics
manufacturers to seek alliances in the hope of regaining their competitiveness in the marketplace. They included another recent
announcement by Philips that it was joining forces with Motorola, the
US group, to design and develop semiconductor chips for Compact
Disk Interactive, a new CD-based medium combining graphics, data,
CD audio and video. The Dutch group is now also looking for a partner
to invest in a plant to manufacture liquid crystal displays, a product of
increasing strategic importance.

ate of similar links has also taken place in Europe's semicon-
or and computer industries over the past year as difficult market
nditions forced companies to adopt measures to stem failing fortunes. Earlier this year Groupe Bull of France, the computer group,
announced a link with IBM of the US to develop advanced semiconductor chips. And SGS-Thomson, the Franco-Italian semiconductor
group is to collaborate with GEC Plessey Semiconductors of the UK
in chip development, and with Philips in a semiconductor plant in
Grenoble. Nokia, the Finnish group, has been restructuring its consumer electronics division, and has also been talking to a number of
unnamed parties about possible links.

Such partnerships have been spurred by the growing recognition
among Europe's indigenous manufacturers that their US and Japanese
competitors could be the main beneficiaries of the single European
market. European electronics companies have accepted they need
help to survive in increasingly competitive markets otherwise they will
not be able to fund the R & D needed to keep pace with technology.
This is particularly true in the semiconductor industry, where most
European companies are suffering losses. 'That is the area in which
European companies are crying out for help,' says Mr Andrew Haskins,
industry analyst at James Capel. Even cash-rich Siemens has realised it
cannot afford the investment needed to stay in the race and recently
announced ventures in chip development with both IBM and Toshiba of
Japan. The move towards alliances follows the failure to build a
European electronics champion through the merger of the semiconductor activities of Siemens, SGS-Thomson and Philips. The three groups
were unable to reconcile their differences and, after months of talks,
Siemens decided to link with IBM, effectively dashing hopes for a major
European electronics group. It is not only that the Europeans find it
difficult to agree on broad co-operation; there has also been a
spreading conviction that simply joining the weak operations of three
big groups will not lead to a strong business. Having abandoned the
idea of a European champion, manufacturers have embraced less
grand alliances, both among themselves and with outside groups, as
the logical solution to their problems. Olivetti has set up a division
specifically to look for possible technological co-operation.

Such alliances offer manufacturers the chance to pool resources and
rationalise operations, at a time of spiralling costs and stagnant growth
of key markets. The situation is particularly dire for financially stretched
European groups. Last year, although Philips returned to profitability, its
income from consumer electronics declined 33 per cent. Thomson,

Nokia and Olivetti also suffered losses last year and the situation is equally bleak among European semiconductor and computer manufacturers. If they are to remain in the race, which means continuing to invest in R & D, Europe's manufacturers need to join forces or seek help from outside. Ms Angela Dean, industry analyst at Morgan Stanley, expects Philips to announce further alliances as it moves to rationalise its operations. 'What we hear from Philips in the future will be more general and not just restricted to video equipment,' she said. Alliances with strategic partners also offer manufacturers the chance to tap demand outside their own national markets. This is important for European manufacturers, which have often blamed their woes on the lack of a large indigenous demand base to support economies of scale. Pan-European alliances will help to rationalise operations and share costs. But they will have limited impact on raising the competitiveness of European manufacturers. For that, European companies will have to look to US and Japanese companies for the key technologies necessary to remain competitive and profitable.

Source: Financial Times, 27 March, 1992

More innovative modern manufacturing enterprises are, then, changing in their operational practices. Their earlier methods of production were rigidly and hierarchically structured with the strategic apex exercising tight control over the operating core through layers of direct supervision. The precise shape and internal dynamics of modern post-Fordist forms of organisation remain uncertain. Equally, issues of strategy formulation and implementation are problematic. In some organisations there appears to be a shift towards strategic decentralisation and the devolution of day-to-day performance responsibilities to a fragmented operating core. It is within such systems that there is the widespread implementation of manufacturing systems based upon 'just-in-time', 'total quality measurement', and 'high performance' work systems. In effect, these require technocrats to relinquish much of their 'monopolised' knowledge and managers in the middle line to allow workers to exercise 'responsible autonomy' rather than being subjected to tight supervisory controls.

ORGANISATIONAL ISSUES

The highly competitive international markets within which manufacturing organisations trade are forcing them to develop fundamentally different practices to those that are considered to be
'Fordist' and steeped in the assumptions of Scientific Management.
Although the demise of 'bureaucracy' and 'Taylorism' has been
grossly overstated, it is evident that advances in information technology, coupled with changing employee expectations, are contributing to a paradigm shift in working practices. The key challenge
for many corporate leaders is to bring about dramatic changes in
both cultures and structures such that innovation and change, working flexibility, team work and trust become features of organisational
reality, rather than just rhetorical slogans which do little but stimulate
deep-rooted cynicism. The extent to which such changes can be
realised is further constrained by broader cultural forces which limit
the extent to which the ideas of F.W. Taylor and Scientific Management can be completely superseded. Accordingly, the death of
standardised and highly routinised work tasks for organisational
members can be far from taken for granted.

5

THE ADMINISTRATIVE ORGANISATION

The growth of large-scale, mass-production manufacturing corporations has been paralleled by the emergence of similar organisational
forms in administrative services. Indeed, a feature of Western economies has been the structural shift of employment from industrial to
administrative sectors. Recently, this trend has been interrupted by
the increasing application of new forms of information technology
in ways which have effectively eliminated a range of routinised work
tasks. But despite such applications, many people continue to be
employed within white collar organisations where large volumes of
highly standardised and repetitive administrative tasks are
co-ordinated. Many of these are public sector organisations, for
example central and local state agencies which monitor, record and
regulate in areas such as taxation, transport, social security, legal
systems and the environment. But there are others with remarkably
similar features which are to be found, more typically, in the private
sector, including, for example, insurance companies, banks and other
related large-scale financial service organisations. Whether publicly
or privately owned, the operating core is essentially concerned with
large-volume data processing using highly regulated and standardised
work processes. This makes them comparable but not identical, in
structural terms, to large-scale manufacturing and consumer service
organisations. But as we shall see, there tend to be differences in
factors such as managerial style, reward systems and corporate culture
which uniquely distinguish administrative organisations.

In general terms, both public and private sector administrative
corporations have attracted considerable criticism over recent years.
They are seen to demonstrate, more than most, many of the alleged
failings associated with bureaucracy; that is, rigidity, narrow-

mindedness, inefficiency, low morale and neglect of customer or end-user preferences. It is undoubtedly the case that many of the features classically associated with bureaucracy – formalisation, specialisation, regulated communication, chains of command, hierarchies of authority and so on – can be most clearly witnessed in administrative organisations. Indeed, what are described as 'full bureaucracies' – combining work flow structuring with formalised personnel procedures – are most commonly found in 'government-owned organisations' (Mintzberg, 1979, p. 331).

But despite the popular association of bureaucracy with 'red tape' and 'inefficiency', there is a large body of management thought which suggests that it represents the most efficient and equitable basis for organisational administration. Indeed, for some observers bureaucracy appears to be an inevitable concomitant of large scale and complexity. Child, for example, asserts that 'So long as most of our work is done in large organisations, we can expect bureaucracy to remain the typical approach to administration' (1977, pp. 209-10). And Perrow remarks, 'in my view bureaucracy is a form of organisation superior to all others we know or can hope to afford in the near and middle future; the chances of doing away with it are probably non-existent in the West this century' (1979, p. 6).

Views such as these derive their intellectual origins from the work of Max Weber, who saw the precision, discipline and reliability of bureaucratic organisations as the most complete expression of rational tendencies within modern capitalist economies. As such, authority relations within bureaucracies differ significantly from other types of organisation. Rules and regulations delineate the rights, obligations and duties of each position within the administrative hierarchy. As a consequence, the bureaucratic official has authority, then, by virtue of position rather than as a result of tradition, personal patronage or reciprocity or charisma. Weber distinguished the following major features of the 'ideal-type' administrative bureaucracy.

Weber's bureaucracy

1 **Specialisation** The work of individuals and departments is broken down into distinct, routine and well defined tasks.
2 **Formalisation** Formal rules and procedures are followed to standardise and control the actions of the organisation's members.

3 **Clear hierarchy** A multi-level 'pyramid of authority' clearly defines how each level supervises the others beneath it.

4 **Promotion by merit** The selection and promotion of staff are based on public criteria (e.g. qualifications or proven competence) rather than on the unexplained preferences of superiors.

5 **Impersonal rewards and sanctions** Rewards and disciplinary procedures are applied impersonally and by standardised procedures.

6 **Career tenure** Job holders are assured of a job as long as they commit themselves to the organisation.

7 **Separation of careers and private lives** People are expected to arrange their personal lives so as not to interfere with their activities on behalf of the organisation.

Source: Handy (1985, p. 192)

Tied together as a coherent whole, these elements constitute the basis of a formally rational organisation which makes possible 'the methodical attainment of a definitely given and practical end by means of an increasingly precise calculation of means' (Pugh, 1979, p. 23). Bureaucratic administration thus facilitates specialisation of individual competencies; operational precision (members know their duties); speed (members know where in the organisation to refer problems, removal of interpersonal friction (individual activities are guided by known rules); and the removal of personal discretion or bias (Sofer, 1973). More generally, the defenders of bureaucracy suggest that it is a guard against nepotism, victimisation and corruption and a force for justice, equality and 'normative integration' (Blauner, 1964).

However, in practice, the application of bureaucratic principles has not always appeared conducive to the promotion of organisational efficiency. Strict conformity to rules, for example, often leads to individual behaviour which can impede the collective achievement of organisational goals. A narrow focus upon job descriptions can limit personal initiative and allow ends (goals) to become obscured by means (procedures). Over the longer term, the career interests of individuals may create barriers within communication processes up and down the hierarchy and lead to the formation of sub-groups which are able to 'manage' rules according to their own vested interests (Crozier, 1964). In such situations the imposition of more rules and tighter regulations is likely to lead only to further conflict and loss of control (Gouldner, 1964; Fox, 1974).

One example of bureaucratic 'dysfunctioning' is provided by Larry Hirschhorn. His analysis reminds us that, despite familiar complaints about bureaucratic red tape, organisational members may willingly 'collude in their own alienation'.

Decision rituals in government agencies

In one agency I consulted to, employees used a *concurrence chain* to develop policies or make decisions. A manager wrote a document proposing a decision or policy and then circulated it to all the other managers on the chain. If they agreed with the document, they signed it; if not, they effectively vetoed it by refusing to sign. The document writer then had to negotiate with each person who did not sign until everyone on the chain approved. Feeling politically exposed people on the chain were cautious in signing any document. On the other hand, feeling burdened and overworked they did not read any document unless it was being put through the concurrence chain. This meant that a manager who wanted attention for any idea had to put it through the chain. Most of management's thinking and communication was thus organized by the chain. Managers began to think like lawyers. They scrutinized documents and [paid] undue attention to wording, fearing that if they signed they might be liable for some mistake later.

The decision process was thus grossly inefficient. Managers could not get an informal hearing for their thinking, nor could they collaborate with a group of colleagues in developing ideas. Both important and insignificant decisions were forced through the chain, leading managers to feel overworked and ineffective. At the same time, since the document writer had to negotiate with each signer separately, final decisions reflected preferences that minimally satisfied everyone, though rarely pleasing anyone. Decision quality degraded. Yet by distributing decision making and accountability over the entire agency the concurrence chain *helped managers deny the primary anxiety of making decisions.* Managers behaved as members of a firing squad, in which everybody shoots but no one knows whose bullet killed the victim. No single person felt accountable and at risk. By depersonalizing the decision process, making it inefficient, and degrading the quality of decisions, managers could feel calm.

Source: Hirschhorn (1988)

In general, it has been argued that the administrative bureaucracy is a form best suited to the management of large-scale units under relatively stable conditions. Where market and environmental circumstances are more volatile and work processes less certain, less specialised, more adaptable forms of organisation may be more appropriate. But it would appear that large-scale bureaucratic organisations may be peculiarly weak at sensing, and responding to, shifts in their environment. Indeed, the history of many public and private sector administrative corporations would indicate their adherence to a set of firmly held assumptions which until recently have remained relatively immune from changing environmental demands. In their most extreme form these core cultural values may be summarised as follows.

Administrative organisations' core cultural assumptions

1 **Consumers** That consumers constitute a largely undifferentiated and unco-ordinated mass whose 'needs' are generally determined by the organisation.
2 **Costs** That costs are unchecked as they will be subsidised in public sector organisations or passed on to the end user/customer.
3 **Competition** That competition is non-existent and that there are high barriers to market entry.
4 **Technology** That technological change is unimportant and unlikely to impact occupational and organisational structures.
5 **Human resources** That employees are compliant/rule-driven and are motivated by secure, long-term organisational careers.
6 **Ownership** That ownership structures are stable and protected by public or private sector quasi-monopoly.
7 **Change** That organisational stability is the normal state and that change is atypical and deviant.
8 **Culture** That operating processes are organised according to tradition, custom and practice and that innovation, adaptiveness and flexibility are disruptive.

In the public sector these assumptions have been undermined by governments intent upon reducing expenditure and increasing the impact of so-called 'market forces' upon state-owned organisations. In the health services throughout the world, for example, the creation of 'internal markets' has established structures based upon 'provider purchaser' relationships, whilst in the administrative civil services, executive agencies have been established to contract – in competition with private suppliers – to deliver services to government departments. As a result, such organisations have been forced to question many of their traditional core values.

According to Flynn (1990) there are four themes which link the reforms brought about in the public sector by the 1980s resurgence of 'new right' or 'new liberal' ideas. These are, first, a preference for market mechanisms as opposed to centralised planning, rationing and allocation. This is evident in the move away from state to personal pensions and, in housing, in the shift from general subsidy to market rents. Second, there is the promotion of competition amongst providers and of choice amongst consumers. Competition is seen as encouraging efficiency and cost reduction, at the same time as promoting customer orientation. Public, private and voluntary providers are increasingly competing for customers in housing, health care and residential provision for the elderly. Third, there is the expansion of opportunities for individual choice in preference to collective decision-making. As a result, the powers of local administrative organisations have been reduced in favour of greater consumer choice in education and housing. Finally, there is the reduction of state provision to certain 'minimum standards' and a focusing upon those who cannot afford to supplement or opt out of such provision altogether. This promotion of self-help denies the automatic link between increasing demand for services such as health and increasing state-funded supply. In other words, those who are wealthy enough to afford services above the minimum should pay directly for it from suppliers of their choice. State organisations should focus their limited resources upon providing safety net services for the less affluent. Whatever the outcome of these shifts – in terms of costs, customer orientation, quality of service as well as broader social and political values – they have undeniably challenged the basic assumptions upon which many post-war public sector administrative organisations have been established, with far-reaching consequences for those managing and working within such organisations.

This has been equally so in the recent history of large-scale administrative organisations in the private sector. The large financial service organisations – banks, building societies and insurance corporations – have also been increasingly exposed to competition mergers and acquisitions throughout the 1980s and 1990s. Some of this competition has come from consumer service businesses, such as the high street food and fashion chains, which can justifiably claim more established retail rather than administrative traditions and practices. This, in turn, has encouraged amongst the established financial giants – rather belatedly, some would argue – a greater appreciation of the personal requirements of customers as well as the need to reduce costs. At the same time the technical capability to deliver – at a low cost – more individually tailored products and services has been made possible by the increasing application of new forms of information technology (Hammer and Champy, 1993). Taken together, these market pressures and technological changes have also combined to deregulate and, in a sense, 'consumerise' large semi-monopolistic administrative organisations in the private sectors of modern economies. If the challenge in state sectors in the 1990s is how to combine a public service ethos with a performance orientation, in private sectors it is achieving cost efficiencies without undermining consumer service. In practice, as we shall see, these dilemmas frequently give rise to similar organisational challenges in terms of structural design and managerial style.

ORGANISATIONAL STRUCTURE AND MANAGEMENT STYLE

In structural terms, administrative service organisations conventionally share many of the characteristics of manufacturing machine bureaucracies. In the post office, insurance company or bank – just as in the car manufacturer or food processing company – work in the operating core tends to be simple, repetitive and routinised. Jobs are tightly and narrowly defined; little room is allowed for individual judgement or discretion. Above the operational process there is often a well-developed and sharply differentiated management hierarchy. Here, first-line supervisors handle any conflicts which may emerge between highly specialised, interdependent operators. Other managers liaise with staff experts in the technostructure and facilitate the flow of information up the hierarchy and the translation of action plans back down. The significance of work procedures, job design, regulations and financial controls ensures that the technostructure is also well developed; as important to the civil service department as it is to the soft drinks manufacturer. Similarly, a shared concern to reduce exposure to environmental incentives encourages both types of organisation to control work processes internally rather subcontract out. Support staff – from the canteen to the reception desk, the industrial relations department to the R & D group – are also well developed. At the very top of these organisations considerable power is centralised in the strategic apex where executive focus conventionally tends to concentrate upon improving existing performance rather than creating new products or services.

Yet such structural similarities do not imply, of course, that manufacturing and administrative organisations are identical. Differing historical origins, technologies, labour markets and ownership patterns have combined to produce distinctive organisational profiles. The predominance of white collar occupations within the operating core of administrative service organisations, for example, is linked with a tradition of employee relations quite distinct from that of large-scale manufacturers. In general, white collar workers, although inclined during the post-war period to join trade unions, are more individualistic in work orientation and acquiescent in their relations with immediate managers. As a result, industrial relations have not been distinguished by the low-trust–high-conflict pattern evident within manufacturing organisations during much of the twentieth century. In addition, at least *some* white collar employees – the semi-skilled, in particular – have experienced upward mobility from the operating core into the middle line in a way rarely available to manufacturing operatives. Other differences arise from the fact that, at least until the early 1990s, when corporations have re-engineered through the widespread application of new technology, the lower levels of administrative organisations have remained highly labour-intensive. Finally, many administrative service organisations – particularly those with regulatory, control and welfare functions which are state-owned – are subject to strict codes of public accountability which powerfully impact job procedures, working relationships and managerial styles.

As a result of these factors, and by contrast to the pluralist cleavages and divisions which characterise many large-scale manufacturing corporations, administrative bureaucracies more often exhibit the features of unitary organisations. Their bureaucratic structures appear to be more widely supported by bureaucratic cultures. The predominant behaviour patterns, attitudes and values of members in all parts of the structure – middle line, operating core, support staff and so on – reflect a shared belief in the fundamentals of bureaucratic administration: the primacy of rules, clear hierarchies, central control and disciplined adherence to procedure. This coincidence of organisational structure and managerial style is discussed below in an earlier study of corporate managers.

Managerial attitudes in administrative bureaucracies

Conformity and risk aversion

'Managers don't necessarily do what they think they should do. They do what they think they ought to do. What will please the organisation . . . I've worked for this organisation for twenty three years and I've been conditioned to its style of thinking and doing. And know their requirements. I know what I should and shouldn't do. Inevitably, it has had a very big influence on my general way of life. . . . The company likes stereotypes.' (General manager, male, early forties.)

'Diplomacy is something which the organisation likes and conformity is an essential ingredient of career progression. . . . you've got to toe the party line. You've got to say the right things at the right time. Looking back over the past twenty years, has it all been worthwhile? The answer is I've got a nice house, a reasonable standard of living . . . I have a family, I'm tied to the business. I earn a decent salary so that compensates for a lot of things.' (General manager, male, early forties.)

Preferred managerial style

Our survey indicated that 'ideas of managerial effectiveness tend to be loosely associated with the structural characteristics of employing organisations. Those in more highly bureaucratised settings are inclined to stress the advantages of more assertive styles while those in other organisational forms are more likely to emphasise more "open" and "consultative" approaches. The tendency for leadership styles and organisational structures to be congruent is possibly derived from features pertaining to the nature of products, technology and skill level of employees (Bryman, 1986). A reliance on rules and procedures is likely to be evident when work processes can be organised for the purposes of providing relatively standardised goods or services for relatively stable markets. Those who are performing such tasks rarely need to exercise personal judgement. Hence, patterns of consultation are likely to be restricted to relatively routine matters.'

Ideal organisational structure

In our survey, managers were asked: 'What, in your opinion, is the most appropriate structure for an organisation in the 1980s?' In the main, men and women's perceptions of organisational effectiveness do seem to be shaped by their immediate work experiences and, hence, reaffirm the subtle interplay between personal styles and prescribed structures. The following comments reflect the preferences of some of those employed in the administrative bureaucracies:

'It is essential to have set lines of communication and accountability. The immediate manager must be known. A subordinate must have one boss. The hierarchy should be pyramid based, with a point at the top. Work must be split between sections . . . without overlap or duplication.' (General manager, female, early forties.)

'A proper central form of administration without which no organisation will function efficiently. Clear lines of communication and responsibility at all levels. Proper and firm direction from senior management.' (Administrative manager, female, late forties.)

'Clear accountability with direct lines of communication to line management.' (Administrative manager, female, late forties.)

'A certain hierarchy of authority is inevitable, but this should be as uncomplicated and clear as possible. Lines of communication and areas of responsibility should be clearly defined and there should be sensible but not excessive delegation.' (General manager, male, early forties.)

Source: Scase and Goffee (1989, pp. 63–4, 71–4)

It is within the context of these deeply ingrained attitudes that the senior executives of both public and private sector administrative service organisations have attempted to introduce change. Needless to say, the process has not been easy. Those who have practised a hierarchical, remote, rule-based style of management do not adapt easily to calls for 'entrepreneurship', 'innovation', 'teamwork' and 'hands-on leadership'. The structural changes associated with this shift in management style typically involve the following:

1 Clear separation of more market-focused, stand-alone business units within the operating core.
2 Day-to-day operational and sometimes strategic control decentralised to the business units.
3 Some functions of the central technostructure and support staff delegated to business units.
4 Some functions of the central support staff contracted out or converted to business-status selling services (in competition with external suppliers) both within the organisation and in the external market.
5 Focusing of central technostructure staff on key indicators of financial performance (and, in some cases, human resource development of high-potential executives).
6 De-layering and slimming of the middle line.
7 Closer, 'hands-on' contact between corporate senior executives and business unit general managers.
8 Focusing of strategic apex on management of strategic portfolio, allocation of resources and establishment of 'rules of the game'.

Taken together, these structural shifts imply a fundamental reshaping of administrative service organisations. Some insight into the implications of such change are provided in the following description of a large Canadian insurance company.

General Insurance: changes in the 1980s

Throughout the 1980s the role of branches had been gradually redefined and expanded so that they could offer customers a total insurance service, instead of operating simply as sales outlets under strict head-office guidelines without the authority to vary the terms of any insurance contract. At the same time, some branches had begun to handle the large commercial customers, whose business was more competitive and potentially more profitable. Greater branch autonomy became necessary, and was encouraged by senior head-office management, until by the mid-1980s the branches had developed into profit centres. The employee handbook stated:

> Each branch is the front-line contact with our existing and prospective policy holders. Branches operate autonomously so

that the particular needs of each area can be identified. Branch managers play an important role in budget planning, so that the targets set are achievable and performance can be measured against the final result.

By 1987 branch managers were writing their own business plans, and settling their own revenue and expense budgets. The new sales orientation also meant that they had to develop new skills, so that they could become active salesmen with a visible presence in the local community. They had to relinquish direct staff supervision, and become field workers servicing in particular the needs of large commercial clients.

The move towards a results-oriented role for branch managers was not triggered by computing developments. But the new direction was supported by computer-generated information that helped branch managers to understand the operation of their business more fully and thus to run their branches autonomously.

Source: Boddy, Buchanan and Patrickson (1991, pp. 155–6)

But of course, very few organisations have implemented all such structural shifts. The differing impact of external pressures, priorities of top managers, attitudes of employees and nature of ownership will influence the rate and extent of change. Although the overall trend is towards decentralisation, there are, nevertheless, a number of factors that will shape the direction of organisational change. According to Flynn (1990) the more important factors that influence the extent of decentralisation in public sector organisations are as follows:

1 **Degree of complexity in work/difficulty in defining outcome**   The greater the complexity, the more difficulty the centre will have in determining and measuring outputs. This has made shifts towards centralisation in education services, for example, difficult to implement.
2 **Degree of consensus on best approach**   The more disagreement there is about the most effective way of running a service, the more central scrutiny is necessary. Differences amongst probation officers, for example, about programmes most likely to produce positive results have limited their development as a self-regulated profession and reinforced the need for central checks on the links between process and outcomes.
3 **Degree of risk associated with failure**   The greater the risk associated with service breakdown, the more the centre must

exercise tight controls over work procedures. If centrally determined procedures for social workers' child care visits are not
properly followed, for example, then the risks to children's lives
may be substantially increased.

Structural change may also be influenced by technological factors.
Indeed, the early applications of new office technology produced a
wave of dramatic predictions about job losses and de-skilling, both in
the operating core and middle line of administrative service organisations. Until the late 1980s, these predictions had proved, in the main,
to be false. Until then, new technology had not led to the elimination of secretarial and clerical positions – although routine data entry
and retrieval jobs (for example, filing and book-keeping) had been
more at risk. Neither had office automation routinely de-skilled
clerical work. Indeed, studies in UK banks and North American
insurance companies indicated, if anything, a neutral or positive
effect in terms of skill levels (Long, 1987).

But by the early 1990s, the picture began to change. Studies in the
US indicated that following an employment peak in 1990, clerical
personnel in the insurance industry would fall by 22%, and in
banking by 10%, by the year 2000 (Long, 1987, p. 123). Further
significant changes were predicted for the shape and size of the
corporate hierarchy:

> All other things being equal, we should see some 'shrinkage' of
> large organisations (in terms of employment) and some flattening
> of the structure, as some hierarchical levels are eliminated.
> Clearly, the number of routine clerical workers in a given
> organisation should decline. In professional/functional areas,
> some semi-professionals will be eliminated.
>
> The supervisory level of the hierarchy could be reduced or
> even eliminated altogether, for several reasons. Fewer lower-level
> workers should require fewer supervisors. Use of the computer
> could eliminate some routine coordinative and surveillance roles,
> while reintegration of jobs, and assumption of some decision
> making by individuals and work groups, possibly aided by the
> computer, could eliminate other roles. As has been described
> earlier, there is some empirical evidence to suggest that
> elimination of a supervisory level can occur.
>
> Reduction of the middle management level might also occur.

Fewer subordinates to supervise, as well as the time savings that could be generated by more efficient communications and the ability to computerise some (although not many) decisions at this level could cause reductions, depending on how top management chooses to utilise the time savings. . . . Middle managers who turn out to be only paper-pushers and information conduits between the top and bottom of the organisation might be eliminated entirely.

(Long, 1989, pp. 208–9)

Dramatic job losses and programmes of corporate restructuring within financial service organisations in the early 1990s suggest that, unlike earlier false alarms, recent predictions have been more accurate. Indeed, a number of recent change initiatives illustrate the central role which can be played by new technology in implementing structural redesign and assisting in strategic re-orientation. Within the administrative service sector a good example is provided by the case of the TSB bank.

Programming the personal banker: TSB

The history of banking has three ages: the age of cartels and assured profits, which ended roughly in 1980; the dawn of competition, when banks scrambled for profits with high-risk strategies that backfired in 1990 or so; and now the age of efficiency, when profits will come from cutting costs and selling low-risk products.

All banks preach a new-age philosophy. It starts from the premise that the high streets are overcrowded; by some reckonings, Britain has twice as many bank and building-society branches as it needs. To survive, banks must slash costs and staff by getting computers to do the paper-shuffling. The branches should be converted into friendly financial shops stocked with an array of profitable, preferably low-risk, services.

That is the theory banks are slowly putting into practice. Britain's TSB (once the Trustee Savings Bank) has made more progress than most . . .

In traditional banking each branch is a fief and each manager a lord. TSB swept away that feudal structure. It demoted its branches (not the language Mr Ellwood would use) by moving much of the clerical work into 70 processing centres. Those centres will do the routine jobs of keeping records and processing cheques. They will also handle all the business customers by telephone and mail. TSB then created a new tier in its hierarchy, senior branches that oversee eight or nine junior ones. Hundreds of managers at junior branches left. Their successors are lower-paid vassals. TSB capped its restructuring by moving all consumer services under the roof of the retail bank.

Cleared of their back offices, the branches can get down to the business of selling financial services. Gone are the filing cabinets and bullet-proof screens (cash is stored in electronically controlled dispensers), in come the "interview bays", where "customer-service executives" ply the bank's wares. Back offices used to occupy three-quarters of the space in TSB's branches; that space is now being used to sell financial products.

Beginning this year, the salesmen will have a nifty new tool: a high-tech vending machine called Superservice, which is supposed to smooth the sale of basic financial services. Salesmen and customers gaze together at a colour computer-screen that instructs them on the virtues of each product, answers questions and spits out an application form for the mesmerised customer to sign. TSB executives claim that, in its trial run, Superservice has boosted by a quarter the number of sales made for every sales pitch. TSB plans to install the system in 1,000 of its 1,500 branches by the end of 1991. Like all TSB machines, Superservice will have immediate access to all information about each customer and will revise that information instantly. That will save the banker hunting for records and the customer droning on about personal details he has had to provide too often before. A clever software system – "expert" in the jargon – does much of the brainwork that a highly-paid loan officer used to do, like suggesting which mortgage to buy and working out how much it will cost. It can even decide whether the customer is a good risk. When TSB's managers want to introduce a new financial product, Superservice will spare them mounting expensive retraining sessions – they can simply put it into the system.

Behind TSB's profit-making gimmickry stands technology borrowed from airline-reservation systems a dozen years ago. All the bank's reps share data about each customer and can revise it instantly. The technology adjusts a customer's balance the moment he pulls cash from a machine or makes a payment on a mortgage. That is what makes it possible for TSB to lump many of its services into regional centres; it also gives the bank a powerful marketing tool. TSB's system can, for example, prompt a cashier to suggest that a customer investigate the virtues of an insurance policy.

To make the most of its machines, TSB's retail division is retraining its

28,000-strong staff. Propaganda bulks large in the curriculum – the catechism of customer service, says Mr Ellwood, "litters our litany". Along with the pep talks, TSB's employees get the skills to sell formerly complicated financial services. The beauty of its system is that anyone with a friendly face and reasonably alert mind can master it. As Mr Ellwood puts it "you don't need three PhDs to lend money". Although the bank relies on higher-trained "consultants" to sell complicated services like pensions, its snazzy technology will cut the age and pay of its sales-force. Machines, it seems, are doing the work of managers as well as clerks. The bank sacked 4,000 staff in 1990, 1,000 of them managers.

Many of TSB's improvements simply follow fashion. Midland Bank, for example, is moving its back-office work into regional processing centres. Barclays, Britain's biggest bank is "clustering" its branches. And Abbey National, formerly a building society, also has the real-time technology that TSB boasts about. Most are paring their staff and retraining the survivors.

TSB's skill has been to orchestrate these elements into a coherent whole. Richard Heygate, a consultant at McKinsey, thinks TSB is among the few companies to solve a problem that has bedeviled service industries for decades: how to use computers to wring extra productivity from their workforces, rather than merely raising costs. TSB's answer is to delegate to these machines the jobs of middle managers as well as of clerks.

Source: The Economist, 20 April 1991

STAFFING ADMINISTRATIVE SERVICE CORPORATIONS: EMPLOYEES AND THEIR REWARDS

Clearly, changes of the kind envisaged by TSB and other financial service organisations have profound implications for the supplier–customer relationship, the skill and knowledge capability of the salesperson and the means by which he or she is managed. Similar shifts have occurred amongst service providers in the public sector. In both contexts there are consequences in terms of preferred employee profiles, appropriate rewards systems and workable career structures. But we should not assume that all administrative service organisations are similar. These points are illustrated in a number of case studies of large, stable, white collar bureaucracies. Crompton and Jones (1984),

Table 5.1   Contrasting human resource strategies in three administrative
service organisations

	Southbank	Lifeco	Cohall
Recruitment	School age	All ages	All ages
Qualifications	Important	Less important	Moderately important
	Bank related	Mixed	Mixed
Formal assessment	Yes	Yes	No
Employer mobility	Very little	Within insurance sector	Moderate
Geographic mobility	High	Low	Moderate
Career orientation	Organisational	Organisational/ occupational	Occupational/ organisational

Source: Crompton and Jones (1984, pp. 81–5)

for example, found considerable variations in human resource profiles of a clearing bank (Southbank), an insurance company (Lifeco) and a local government authority (Cohall) (see Table 5.1).

On the basis of this evidence it would seem that local government managers are more able to pursue occupational careers, with potential to transfer their abilities and expertise across a range of organisational contexts. Managers in the banks and, to a lesser extent the insurance companies, more typically have organisational careers which tend to evolve through lengthy service for a single employer and which place considerable emphasis upon 'loyalty', 'reliability' and 'commitment'. Some insight into the attitudinal impact of this type of strong, internal labour market, both within the middle line and, significantly, at the strategic apex, is provided in the following description of career systems within a major retail clearing bank.

The basic system of staff management had been stable in the bank since the inter-war years. An entrant to the bank, particularly a male entrant, could expect a lifetime career starting as a sixteen year old school-leaver doing a teller's job in a local branch, progressing through a range of 'back office' jobs and set of Institute of Bankers' exams. Movement to other branches preceded appointment to supervisor, and success in this role would lead to appointment as Assistant Branch Manager,

107

then Branch Manager. Promotion was almost entirely from within. Together with the other UK clearing banks, Midland operated an informal cartel which prevented recruitment of each other's staff. Many benefits, such as cheap mortgages, were service-related. Promotion tended to be on line manager's recommendations.

Executives in the 1970s had tended to come through this background. As one General Manager remarked: 'Most of the top executives in the bank today were recruited as clerks from grammar schools, with "O" or "A" levels. They wanted a good solid job and came from families where parents emphasized virtues such as conformity and loyalty. Often their fathers were in banking jobs.'

(London Business School case study, prepared by Tim Morris and Paul Willman, 1991)

Clearing banks in the private sector and, plausibly, civil service departments in the public sector perhaps represent the most extreme form of an administrative culture within which the central bond between employee and organisation has been the bureaucratic career. The 'psychological contract' has been essentially as follows: job security in return for organisational commitment; job progression (promotion through the hierarchy) in return for loyalty and (certificated) merit. In a sense, the ideology of the managers in middle line has pervaded these organisations, encouraging – in the view of their strongest critics – an introverted obsession with hierarchy and procedure, often to the neglect of end-user/customer requirements and associated longer-term corporate goals.

In this context, the structural shifts outlined in the previous section represent a cultural shock. In the absence of sudden and massive labour turnover or substitution, restructuring directly affects levels of job satisfaction, career goals and, indeed, life ambitions amongst existing employees. An index of this is provided in the profile we present below of survey data we collected in an earlier study of a number of major organisations, including a large clearing bank.

Reluctant managers

In 1989 we completed a survey of 375 men and women managers employed within a range of large-scale UK-based organisations (see

Case study table 1.1). We described many as 'reluctant managers', 'less than fully committed to their jobs and with great reservations about giving priority to their work, their careers and, indeed, their employing organisations. They are more careful, perhaps, than in the past about becoming "psychologically" immersed in their occupations and seek, instead, to obtain a balance between their work and private lives. They are reluctant to strive for career success if this can be gained only at the expense of personal and family relationships. Consequently, they are less prepared to subordinate their personalities to the requirements of their work and careers . . . (they) feel they are subject to "excessive" pressures and query whether the rewards are worth the effort; if their employing organisations cannot guarantee

Case study table 1.1 Survey of 375 men and women managers employed within a range of large-scale organisations

	Bank (%)	Other organisations (%)
Employer dependency		
Always worked for this employer	83	25
Worked for this employer 20 yrs+	52	25
University level qualifications	6	25
Experience of unemployment/ redundancy	4	14
Housing benefits	96	33
Partner relations		
Wife in employment	39	68
Wife's role primarily domestic	89	61
Workload and job satisfaction		
Working week up in last 5 years	69	50
Reduction in work time welcomed	70	46
Technological change increases stress	69	52
Personal satisfaction of work is exaggerated	63	37
Career/life orientation		
Major source of satisfaction in life is		
My job	4	13
My career	2	20
My family	78	52
I anticipate blocked career	57	22
Chance and luck determines career success	65	39
Choose different career if starting again	50	29

security and promotion prospects, why should they, in turn, be prepared to invest themselves *fully* in their jobs?'

Source: Scase and Goffee (1989, 179–180)

Male managers, locked into middle line jobs in a clearing bank, represent the most extreme example of the reluctant manager syndrome.

Reluctant managers feel locked into organisations where they are 'going nowhere'. Escape routes are blocked by their lack of transferable skills and inexperience of other types of employment. If partners are not in employment and there is a dependent family, then the trap is complete. Dissatisfied and disillusioned, they invest the minimum effort required to retain their jobs and transfer most of their energies outside the workplace – into leisure pursuits, family activities and so on. In the most extreme cases, these managers create distractions for themselves at work by undermining others' efforts and political gameplaying. The role model they present to others can be devastating in its consequences for corporate morale.

Reluctant managers represent one of the most important human resource issues facing administrative service organisations today. Senior executives frequently express concern about the loss of high-potential 'stars'; but the retention of large numbers of demotivated middle managers can create even more anxiety. Few organisations seem to have faced up to the challenge of redesigning reward systems and career paths in ways which will win back the commitment of their longer-serving employees for whom promotion is no longer an option. The starting point in most cases involves careful counselling and, often, retraining. Thereafter, the possibilities of job redesign and lateral transfers can be explored, together with options for shifting reward packages to emphasise performance and productivity rather than promotion and prospects.

In the absence of initiatives in such areas, administrative service organisations may find it increasingly difficult to attract younger people with appropriate talents into their employment. The sons and daughters of civil servants, local authority employees or bank managers are unlikely to choose similar careers in the 1990s having seen, at first hand, the increasing uncertainties experienced by their parents during the 1970s and 1980s. The limited appeal of these organisations may be further reduced by implicit and explicit themes within corporate cultures which have systematically blocked the progress of women and ethnic minority groups. Whereas the operating core and lower middle line of many administrative bureaucracies have large numbers of these groups, the upper middle line and strategic apex has typically remained a white, male enclave. Indeed, the emergence of these separate labour markets can seriously undermine the 'unitary' traditions which in the past have often distinguished administrative service from manufacturing organisations.

More generally, the continuing requirement – particularly in public sector administrative organisations – for procedural controls and regulations may restrict the impact of organisational change initiatives. These themes are explored in the case example below.

Middle management experiences of devolution in Barsetshire County Council Social Services Department

Barsetshire County Council (BCC) is one of the larger English county councils, employing over 28,000 employees, and providing services for a large mixed urban/rural area with about a million inhabitants. BCC has enthusiastically adopted the organisational and managerial changes advocated by central government, frequently pioneering new initiatives in advance of legislative requirements.

Speaking about the requirements for change, the chief executive explained that 'There was very little true management thinking. The organisation was dominated by a professional ethos – a very strong professional ethos, and a very excellent one – but I decided it was necessary to introduce a more business-like approach, bringing together the strength of a *professional* ethos within the delivery of services with the *management* of resources'.

Key features of these organisational changes included:

- a coherent strategic planning system, involving business planning for each service
- a strong leadership style through the authority, embodying core BCC beliefs and values
- personnel management changes, including more flexible (fewer and wider) job grades, performance review system and performance-related pay

- organisational restructuring, including a flatter structure with reduced management layers
- a culture change, replacing 'administration' by a culture based on devolved management, by reducing bureaucracy and 'red tape' and by reducing the hierarchical structure.

Devolved management in the Social Services Department (SSD) during the late 1980s and into the 1990s, involved two key aspects – devolution from the SSD Centre at County Hall to the six geographical areas, and, within each of the areas, the line managers. The BCC chief executive envisaged devolved management in terms of devolving power and control to line managers, as far down the organisational hierarchy as possible, over resources such as finance, personnel, and information etc., within a specified organisational framework of clearly understood accountabilities and limits of authority. When asked for their own under-standing of the term, some middle managers' views corresponded almost exactly with those of the chief executive.

> It has certainly meant greater responsibility and accountability for what you are doing. You do have greater freedom within the parameters of good practice, guidance, regulations and financial control – you are not continually having to ask the person above you for something so there is a cultural shift.
>
> (Locality Manager, Children and Families)

All of the managers attached great significance to being given greater control over their budgets. But many managers, whilst acknowledging the greater extent of their control and responsibilities, queried the extent of the constraints, some to the point where they felt very little had changed:

> I'm tempted to say very little in real terms – I don't think devolution in our department is genuine. Devolution for me is putting accountability down the line saying to people 'This is yours – you get on with it with the costs and the benefits'. I don't see much evidence of that really happening. One example: devolved financial accountability. But it doesn't actually amount to: 'Here's your budget; do what you like with it'. The systems are supposed to allow people to act in an independent way but this really barely exists. I think the financial management systems are really heavily bureaucratised themselves. This is where the conflict comes in. There's this sort of, on the one hand, entrepreneurial spirit, you know – 'go out and do all these things' and yet it's 'oh, you can't

do that because these procedures say you must do this, that and the other'.

(Assistant General Manager, Children and Families)

Several managers were very positive about the way in which the devolved management system gave them the opportunity to focus more specifically on the needs of the client – to develop needs-based rather than resource-led services. The prospect of competing with the private and voluntary sector on the service provisions side, under the purchaser/provider split, had also made it necessary to define more sharply the most cost-effective way of providing them. Some managers also commented on the limits to their powers here, explaining that their discretion over service provision decisions was exercised within fairly restricted margins, circumscribed by requirements to get authorisation from their line managers, by the increasing volume of both national legislation and BCC's own procedures, and by decreasing resource allocation (both finance and staff).

> I think that devolution is down to accountability, and hence standards of accountability. I think that we are pretty well prescribed in what we do; there are a lot of rules and regulations – child protection, really, the Children's Act – child protection procedures . . . and with care management coming in (under the Community Care Act) there are going to be quite firm guidelines there.

(Service Manager, Children and Families)

Increased control by line managers over resources such as property, information, finance and personnel, within a clearly specified corporate framework, was a key feature of the authority's devolved management system. Most of the managers felt that they had acquired increased decision-making responsibilities for their financial resources through devolved budgeting, which was enhanced by the introduction of a computerised financial management system.

However, many managers felt that their budgetary discretion was limited in practice to small marginal sums, because the vast majority of their funds was already allocated from providing statutory (compulsory) services over which there was little discretion, and for staff costs, which left little room for manoeuvre overall. Moreover, money could be removed from their budgets, at the behest of the centre, to cover overspending in another SSD area. The scope for practices such as viring between budgets heads, carrying money forward, etc. was also extremely limited – by regulations, by requirements to obtain authorization, and ultimately, by political/legal constraints:

> I seem to be constantly writing memos to either my line manager, or the commissioner (the purchaser), or the area director, telling him we want to do something, and how much it's going to cost, and asking him if it is okay to do it. Politically, you have to be quite careful about borrowing between the client groups. Traditionally, adult services have been used to bolster up children and family services, but you can't take that decision locally; that has to go up through the system and so you are a bit restricted. There's probably a limit to real devolution in local government because of the political accountability and democracy thing.
>
> (Assistant General Manager, Children and Families)

As part of the devolution process, many central personnel, finance and information systems specialist staff were moved out from the centre of the line managed by the service departments; they had a diagonal or 'dotted line' relationship, as BCC put it, with their head of profession at the centre in County Hall. This move was designed to encourage the staff to provide a service more directly geared towards these departments' business or service provision needs, rather than acting as centralised, remote and controlling millstones around the necks of these service departments.

Several of the managers felt that the relationship had become more of a partnership:

> I think they may be trying to think that way. They are providing you with something that they are more specific about, they are increasingly asking what you want from them . . . there is much more thought given to what we require and what they can offer, and making something out of it between us, and them, being responsive to our needs as well. I mean there is a long way to go on it certainly, but it's starting.
>
> (Locality Manager, Children and Families)

The managers were asked whether they were generally positive or generally negative about the impact of devolution on their work overall. The majority expressed extremely positive views, commenting on the increased job satisfaction and more challenging work arising from the additional responsibilities. Also highlighted were the increased accountabilities and greater responsiveness to client and community needs, and greater awareness of the costs of services, which combined with clearer planning systems, enabled scarce resources to be targeted more effectively to areas of greatest need.

Whilst agreeing with some of the benefits noted above, some managers remained essentially sceptical about the process, feeling that they had been given additional responsibilities, but insufficient real authority or decision making powers.

Source: Keen (1994 pp. 137–47, *Passim*)

ORGANISATIONAL ISSUES

Whether in private or public sector, large-scale administrative service organisations face similar managerial problems. A concern to balance public service with performance and customer service with cost efficiencies has produced similar tensions. Structural shifts and the application of new technology reflect the preoccupation of senior managers with these dilemmas. But the pace of change will be limited by the strong administrative traditions of such organisations. For example, in recent public sector reorganisations, hasty attempts to impose more task-orientated, flexible operating procedures have sometimes led only to confusion and 'inefficiency'. This, in turn, has been 'fixed' by the reimposition and tightening of formal controls and operating procedures! Radical change within such organisations will only be sustained if this familiar vicious cycle can be broken.

6

TRENDS IN THE CONSUMER
SERVICE ENTERPRISE

As living standards have increased in the western economies during the post-war era, the consumption of services of all kinds has grown dramatically. More and more people have been able to buy goods and services previously considered the privilege of a wealthy minority. Expenditure on homes, household goods, travel, tourism, hotels and restaurants, and on a wide variety of leisure and sporting activities, has risen rapidly. Even shopping itself has been marketed as a leisure activity as the services offered by retailers have become increasingly sophisticated. Some of these consumer services continue to be provided by very small-scale, locally-based organisations – as we discussed in Chapter 1 there has been a resurgence of entrepreneurial activity in the service sector over recent years. But despite the relative fragmentation of the sector – certainly by comparison to manufacturing – consumer services are increasingly delivered, for most people, most of the time, by large national and international corporations. In other words, retailing and the provision of various consumer services has become big business.

The emergence of large-scale consumer service corporations follows a lengthy – and continuing – period of rationalisation and restructuring. Within retailing, for example, this occurred first in the grocery sector, but over recent years other types of retail provision have become more concentrated. With growth, retail operations have also become increasingly international. During the 1980s, continental European chains such as Benetton and Ikea came to the UK, whilst Marks and Spencer, Laura Ashley and Body Shop expanded both in Europe and North America. A similar pattern of internationalisation was evident in other consumer service sectors such as hotels, fast food chains, travel and tourism, involving, for example, Holiday Inn,

Intercontinental, Novotel, McDonald's and Grand Metropolitan. As in other sectors, large-scale consumer service corporations benefit from economies of scale. This increases buying power with suppliers, enabling them to centralise administrative activities and providing them with the resources for funding new ventures and product development. In addition, their dominance in the market place often helps them to manipulate barriers to entry, to determine market trends, and therefore to minimise competition. There are also economies of replication derived from the uniform application of standards across all outlets.

With this growth in scale and centralisation, the role of senior management in formulating strategy has increased significantly (Sparks, 1989). In retailing, there are clearly identifiable, centrally driven strategies of segmentation, diversification and niche market franchising. But despite these different strategies, all large-scale corporations within this sector share a number of organisational challenges. Consumer service operations are distinguished by their labour intensiveness as well as by direct contact between employee and customer which, in turn, represents an important part of the 'service experience'. How, then, do these corporations provide, on a mass scale, high-quality but affordable services? For the most part, as we have seen in other sectors, the achievement of consistency has involved the progressive bureaucratisation of work processes. But to what extent can work be standardised and, indeed, mechanised in service provision? What if the pursuit of profit, efficiency and cost effectiveness ultimately renders personal service entirely *im*personal? Consumers, after all, can choose to provide these services for themselves or revert to the more personalised services of smaller enterprises. It is because of these tensions that the contemporary application of new technology within large-scale service corporations may not always be directly linked with productivity increases – at least as this is conventionally understood within manufacturing organisations.

Checking out at Sainsbury's

Mrs Christine Wharton smiles at a shopper in J.Sainsbury's supermarket in Stevenage as she passes her goods across the laser scanner of her till and places them in a plastic bag. A packet of frozen beans takes 5 seconds, a carton of yoghurt 1.2 seconds. The smile is not measured. Mrs Wharton is operating one of six tills being tested at the store in Hertfordshire which allow the operator to pack shopping as well as scan it. The till reduces her output by a third: she scans fourteen items a minute instead of twenty-one. But young parents and older shoppers like these tills, and the company is to install more. As Sainsbury has expanded over the past 10 years, the speed at which its employees process items has steadily fallen. More people have been hired to staff instore delicatessens, bakeries and cigarette kiosks. More of their time is taken up by training. Shelf packers are told to respond more readily to "customer interference" – shoppers asking for help. Sainsbury's experience is typical of Britain's service industries. Although the value of goods handled by each Sainsbury employee has risen by three per cent a year, it and other service companies have not matched the increase in productivity seen in British manufacturing in the past decade. As output has risen in retailing and hotel and catering, the service has become more complex and the number of staff has grown. The thirst for staff created by increasing quality of service is one reason why retailers have lagged behind manufacturers in measured productivity growth. Hotels and restaurants have been even more cautious about automation. Customers will pay more to be served well; machines cannot cook food or clean rooms as well as people. "We are not like Ford. The last thing we want is to get up to a speed on the tills that makes the customers feel they are being chucked through", says Mr Stuart Carter, Sainsbury's district manager for the Stevenage store.

Source: Financial Times, 4 April, 1990

ORGANISATIONAL STRUCTURE AND MANAGEMENT STYLE

Sainsbury, the leading UK food retailer, employs over 120,000 people and has grown to become one of the largest corporations in Europe. In 1993 it ranked 39 in terms of market capitalisation ($11,694m.) and had a turnover of $14,774m. Alongside it in the retail sector are Marks and Spencer, ranked 22 in market capitalisation ($16,381m.) with a turnover of $9,077m. and 62,000 employees; and Tesco, ranked 95 in market capitalisation ($5,907m.), with a turnover of $11,564m. and 86,000 employees. In the hotel and catering sector, Forte is one of the largest in Europe with a turnover of $4,150m. market capitalisation of $2,935m. and 81,000 employees (FT500, 1994).

Each of these businesses has experienced remarkable growth and prosperity over the past two decades. In terms of their management systems and corporate organisation they are seen to be at the leading edge of their respective sectors. Yet despite their size and sophistication, each of them remain, in a sense, family businesses. In terms of both control and, to a lesser extent, ownership there are continuing links between today's senior executives and the founding families. As such, decision-taking processes and management style bear the distinctive stamp of the original owners. To some extent this is a result of their very rapid expansion from private family enterprises to publicly quoted corporations during a relatively short period. But it also reflects the distinctive environment of retailing, where speed of response and limited time spans on many management decisions favour tight, centralised strategic and financial control.

Centralisation v. decentralisation in consumer services

In our sample of companies we have, with minor exceptions, two camps. At the one extreme are the decentralists, who operate as federations of independent small units. At the other end are the centralists, who have large functional departments at headquarters and very limited autonomy at operating level. With one exception, the centralists are all retailers . . .

"We are selling consistency", says Sir John Sainsbury. "The customer has to feel familiar with the layout and goods offered in any of our stores, wherever they are in the country." The whole sales pitch is based on the customer's knowledge that the packet of frozen peas he buys in Lancashire will be the same quality and value for money wherever he goes within that shopping chain. So the key areas where the retailers maintain central control include design, presentation, stock and pricing, as well as more commonplace areas such as capital expenditure . . .

The other strongly centralised company in our sample is Trusthouse Forte. "Central control has made this business what it is," declares Rocco Forte . . . within, say, the hotel division, the areas of responsibility delegated to the individual hotel manager are severely constrained. Decisions on pricing, advertising, decor and capital investment all tend to be taken at divisional headquarters. "Our business is all about maintaining standards," says Lord Forte. Unless you have direct control, that's very hard.

Source: Goldsmith and Clutterbuck (1985, pp. 29–30)

Consumer service organisations – retailers are the best examples – co-ordinate their activities primarily through tight, centrally determined work systems and procedures. These, in turn, are reinforced by systematic and rigorous direct supervisory control mechanisms. Within typically strict parameters regarding price and merchandise mix, the role of the local unit manager focuses almost entirely upon the maximisation of sales and the control of costs. The direct, face-to-face involvement of senior executives within some of the best-known companies is well known. Rocco Forte, chief executive of the Forte hotel chain, argues that 'the more people at the centre sit back and let one person tell them about each area, the less in touch they are. I walk into an hotel and I can see straight away how it is being kept. It makes me aware of problems long before they appear in the figures' (Goldsmith and Clutterbuck, 1985, p. 15). In the US, retail executives such as Bill Marriott and Sam Walton have also stressed the significance of 'getting into the field'; both said they spent at least half their time there. The close involvement of senior executives in the day-to-day detail of retail activities tends to pervade the entire culture of such organisations, as the case of Marks and Spencer illustrates.

Marks and Spencer

The management systems of Marks and Spencer – the leading UK retailer of clothes, foods and homeware – was described by one observer in the early 1980s in the following terms:

> Systems are strongly centralised and controlled from Baker Street, which determines in detail what stores will sell and at what price. Within their defined spheres of responsibility, senior managers act quickly, decisively and with unquestioned personal authority. Speed of reaction is critical . . . senior directors, notably the Chairman, have a marked influence on decisions at all levels. In part this is formal – through Board meetings, departmental reviews and so on. But decisions are just as likely to result from

a chance meeting or a visit, from a small directorial statement or from some event which happens to come to senior attention. Anything at Marks and Spencer is liable to become 'political' at any moment, especially at Baker Street. In this sense a distinction between the strategic and the operational is difficult to maintain.

(Howells, 1981, pp. 338–9)

Lord Sieff, Chairman of Marks and Spencer during the 1980s, described his management style in the following way:

One of the ways in which I implemented my policy was by making more visits to stores and suppliers. . . . We were and still are a centralised business, though we listen carefully to our store divisional executives' and store management's suggestions for improvement; but it was the responsibility of the executives at head office to decide on the catalogue we ran, the new lines we introduced, the lines to be eliminated, production programmes and the amounts to be distributed to each store. . . . My normal week began with the Monday morning meeting of directors; then I had informal conversations with top executives, followed by visits to a number of the merchandise departments to look at the current and developing range of goods. Every week I looked at the sale of new trial lines of clothing, foodstuffs and goods in other departments and listened to recommendations from my colleagues: whether the lines should be developed for national distribution or continued for the moment as trials, or, based on poor initial sales and store comments, eliminated immediately.

Then there were meetings with our suppliers – some in Baker Street, some at their factories – and visits to our stores throughout the country. These were generally on Thursdays, Fridays and Saturdays. . . .

I opened each Monday meeting with an account of what I had seen in the stores the previous week. I put the emphasis upon what was wrong, rather than what was right.

(Sieff, 1988, pp. 273–4)

This type of managerial style encourages all employees - not just the managers – to act as the 'eyes, ears and brains' of the organisation. At store level, all sales staff have a part to play in watching customers, testing merchandise and anticipating trends. Senior managers visiting the stores probe in detail on sales movements and product quality and report back swiftly on their observations. According to one writer with first-hand experience, the management style is 'visible, assertive, sharp and demanding of high standards and effort' (Howells, 1981, p. 347). Any deviance from centrally determined standards or commonly perceived 'core values' is swiftly detected and corrected.

The standards, procedures and systems which shape work processes within large-scale service organisations are developed centrally by a variety of technical specialists. The standards produced by these large and sophisticated technostructures apply to areas such as pricing, product design, raw material specifications, store/unit layout, recruitment, staff presentation and so on. As such, they determine in fine detail the actions of suppliers and employees alike. Indeed, the technostructure represents the key part of these organisational structures, since technical specialists gain power at the expense of retail assistants and operatives, whose work they standardise and measure continuously, and managers, whose co-ordinating functions are effectively transferred into the systems which they design. Certainly, the scope for discretion for those either employed within or supplying such organisations is severely constrained. The logic of industrial production, founded upon the principles of Scientific Management, has been applied to consumer service corporations with some dramatic results, as the example of McDonald's illustrates.

Setting standards at McDonald's

McDonald's lays much stress on the high quality and consistency of its products and goes to great lengths to ensure that a Big Mac, for example, tastes the same all over the world, whether it is sold in Los Angeles, London, Tokyo or Hong Kong. To achieve this end, the company lays down strict specifications as to the manufacture of the products sold in its restaurants, enforced by continuous quality control checks, while restaurant staff are required to follow to the letter the step by step cooking procedures established by the company. Much of the preparation process is controlled by machines, with, for example, an automated meat timer telling the 'grill person' precisely when to turn the hamburger patties and with milk shakes and soft drinks being dispensed at the touch of a button. This highly automated, virtually foolproof preparation system means that a uniform standard can be maintained by staff with a minimum of training and expertise, and so means considerable cost savings on the whole operation – a capital intensive approach . . . . To ensure that the distinctive taste of the McDonald's bun was faithfully reproduced, baking equipment formerly used in West's (US supplier) Norwalk plant was shipped to the UK and only Manitoba hard red spring wheat is used to produce the flour from which the buns are made.

Source: Eurofood, 28 August, 1980

In summarising the impact of the standardised production of the 'technocratic hamburger' at McDonald's, Theodore Levitt proclaims, in a classic article, that, 'the owner has no discretion regarding what he can sell . . . and the employees have virtually no discretion regarding how to prepare and serve things. Discretion is the enemy of order, standardisation and quality' (1972, pp. 41, 52).

Like other so-called machine bureaucracies, then, large consumer service organisations have well-developed, centralised techno-structures and support staff. But they are typically distinguished, in structural terms, by a relatively flat hierarchy and a widely dispersed operating base made up of numerous outlets.

Consumer service organisations are characterised by two distinctive and largely separate labour markets. On the one hand, there are line managers, technical and professional staff and on the other there are those engaged in customer delivery and service who undertake relatively routinised and semi-skilled work. The growth of service organisations has led to the emergence of distinctive, centrally driven strategies and operating standards and, as a result, head office staff are responsible for specialist functions such as strategic planning, forecasting, financial management, sales, merchandising, customer liaison, research, technical standards and computer systems. These offer either support services to senior executives, line managers and operatives, or produce and assess the standards which shape the nature of work processes, skills, products and services within distribution and retail outlets.

Such functions are staffed primarily by graduates, often recruited direct from university. In some cases, though not all, subsequent career paths are concentrated entirely within head office. This can lead to a number of problems:

The first is that they pose a threat to older, perhaps non-graduate staff who have traditionally formed the backbone of management in such organisations . . . .The second problem is that such staff develop high expectations at recruitment which may, if frustrated, lead to high turnover later on. The third is that a large graduate entry programme creates a career block for those who enter retailing organisations as school-leavers on a permanent basis.

(Willman, 1989, p. 15)

These problems may be mitigated by the careful movement of graduate specialists between head office and stores. In Marks and Spencer, for example, the early career path of merchandisers involves substantial exposure at store level before joining a head office buying team. As many retailers have found, however, opportunities for this kind of mobility may be more restricted within some other specialist groups such as computer services. Indeed, a prolonged tour of operational roles may actually exacerbate the career frustrations of graduates looking for rapid promotion. Amongst store managers the situation can be rather different. Since consumer service organisations typically operate across a very large number of relatively small outlets, a sizeable number of both general and specialist managers at local unit level is always a necessity. Such management positions, responsible for sales, stock control, customer relations and personnel, have traditionally been filled by non-graduates. Indeed, this part of the service sector has generally offered managerial career routes to those who, with few qualifications, have been excluded from opportunities within large-scale administrative and manufacturing organisations.

A survey of managers employed in a large UK leisure services organisation showed they differed from those in other sectors, in a number of ways (Scase and Goffee, 1989). Even though they were younger than managers in other sectors (80 per cent were aged between twenty-five and forty-five), they were less well educated. Less than 10 per cent had a first degree, by comparison to over 25 per cent in comparable industrial manufacturing companies. Salary levels were also lower, even though a substantial proportion held general management positions. Perhaps of most significance, many saw themselves as trapped in career terms. To an extent this reflected the flatness of organisational design and the limited career routes between operating unit and headquarters. In response to these career frustrations, managers were more liable either to move to other employers or to start their own businesses. Indeed, the survey showed almost 80 per cent had given serious thought to the latter option, by comparison to 55 per cent in other non-retail organisations.

Consumer service organisations are often able, then, to provide early general management exposure to a large proportion of their younger, relatively less well educated staff. In the long run, however, it frequently proves difficult to sustain career paths, although the largest corporations are at least able to promote people from smaller to relatively large operating units. More generally, the consumer service sector, polarised between the large multiple chains on the one hand and a diverse spread of small retail outlets on the other, sustains a culture of entrepreneurship which influences managerial styles and career choices. So long as operations remain labour-intensive, start-up capital requirements are likely to be low; in this context managers' ambitions to run an independent business have more chance of being fulfilled than in most other sectors (Scase and Goffee, 1987b).

But what of working conditions and rewards for those working within the operating core of the large service corporations? There are typically significant numbers of staff performing tasks where the scope for discretion and responsibility is minimal. As work processes have become increasingly subdivided, routinised and mechanised, skill requirements have diminished. This so-called de-skilling process has had far-reaching consequences. In restaurants, for example, highly trained chefs with considerable autonomy have been replaced by kitchen operatives whose work is closely prescribed, on the one hand by rigorously standardised recipes and, on the other, by freezer and microwave cooking technology. In retailing, giant supermarkets and hypermarkets have become staffed predominantly by shelf-stockers, loaders, cutters, checkout assistants. Amongst these employees, knowledge of the products which they process and sell or, indeed, of the customers whom they serve, may be sparse and often non-existent. Such jobs have low status, low pay, few career prospects and high levels of insecurity. They typically require little or no training. Indeed, they are frequently designed so that almost anyone can do them, with minimal time wasted in getting up to speed. But clearly it is not anyone that fills these jobs. It tends to be those with severely limited opportunities in the labour market who, in the absence of alternatives, are constrained to working in low-skill service occupations. Those who are poorly educated, the young, ethnic minorities, migrant groups and, increasingly, women – employed on a part-time basis – are heavily over-represented within the operating core of large-scale service corporations. Indeed, the overwhelming predominance of distinct social groupings in some job categories has led some observers to describe them as 'occupational ghettoes' – areas of employment categorised by low pay, insecurity and lack of opportunity.

There is a mass of evidence to show that all jobs – whether or not they are in the service sector – which are devoid of skill, variety or autonomy can reduce levels of job satisfaction and lower the involvement and commitment of staff. Those who manage such staff may often, in turn, perceive low levels of employee involvement as 'evidence' that such employees may not be trusted. Pressures then evolve to make work tasks even more regulated and prescribed, generating a downward spiral of the low-trust–low-discretion syndrome (Fox, 1974). However, narrow, routinised and highly structured jobs do not always produce high levels of job dissatisfaction. A common error of many observers of such work has been to assume that their own sources of satisfaction are shared by those they observe. Highly educated professionals may value independence and freedom of expression, and occupations which embrace these values will enhance their feelings of personal development and lead to high levels of job satisfaction. But for many, employment is not perceived as a vehicle for personal growth and self-development. Instead the need for financial rewards, security, friendship and working with others can be the major sources of job satisfaction (Hunt, 1992). Of course, it is possible that expectations of employees are primarily a function of labour market realities. Hence, employee expressions of job 'satisfaction' can not be taken at face value and as 'proof' that they are not, fundamentally, alienated from their employment.

The recruitment and selection practices of most large-scale service corporations indicate a preference for staff with relatively limited work expectations. Once employed, two contrasting managerial strategies may be distinguished whereby centrally determined standards amongst such staff are implemented. The first, associated with the low-cost recruitment of the cheapest labour, relies heavily upon enforcing explicit and external standards of performance. A mixture of formalised controls and close face-to-face supervision is used to induce poorly paid and largely untrained employees to adopt the appropriate forms of behaviour. There are, however, many costs associated with such an approach, including poor manager–staff relations, low commitment, conformity, lack of initiative and high levels of labour turnover. It can also lead to higher managerial costs because of the need for extensive rules and procedures, excessive layers of supervision and a disproportionate amount of management time devoted to job descriptions, the determination of performance standards and so on. But perhaps the biggest problem relates to the implications of such management styles for staff–customer relations. Employees with low levels of corporate commitment and limited attachment to operating standards are unlikely to provide good service delivery. It is for precisely these shortcomings – highlighted by competitors who have been able to provide and reward demonstrably better service with more highly motivated employees – that a number of established service enterprises have suffered a significant loss of market share during the 1990s. The persistence of such a style in some organisations may stem from a number of factors. Monopolistic suppliers of services may, of course, be insulated from the need to upgrade quality of service provision. At the same time, state sector service monopolies may lack the resources necessary to attract higher-quality staff or to invest in their training and development. Finally, some employers may opt for the 'low-cost' enforcing strategy primarily because employee–customer contacts are perceived to be relatively unimportant, being neither extensive nor complex. In such circumstances it may be argued that overall customer satisfaction is determined more by the quality of the products delivered – furniture in a retail store, rooms in a hotel, food in a restaurant – than by the quality of the human labour which delivers them.

A second strategy, associated with the employment of relatively well-paid and trained staff, relies more upon internalising standards of performance. Such an approach involves extending to 'non-career' staff within the operating core the kind of benefits and rewards normally confined to managerial staff (Pfeffer, 1994). There are five characteristic elements of a 'high involvement' human resources policy in consumer service organisations. First, considerable resources are allocated to employee training, not only during the induction period but at regular intervals – on and off the job – throughout employment. As such, training is seen not merely as a means of imparting certain narrow technical skills, it is also a way of encouraging workers to 'take pride and responsibility for a mundane job' (Peters and Waterman, 1982, p. 255). Training, then, represents a means by which managers are able to communicate those behaviours and values which must be consistently and rigorously applied across business operations; it is, in effect, a device for employee socialisation. Some consumer service organisations, such as the John Lewis Partnership and Key-mart, have always practised this strategy, while others, such as British Airways and SAS, have rediscovered the significance of training, particularly for customer service purposes – and invested heavily in it – as part of their corporate programmes during the 1980s and 1990s.

Second, investment in training is supported, as it traditionally has been in many Japanese corporations, by human resource policies which encourage long-term employment. In a sector marked generally by low levels of job security and high levels of labour turnover, employers offering more secure jobs aim to attract and develop higher-quality staff. Many are able to protect the job security of full-time employees by using casual, part-time and sub-contract labour as a buffer against downturns in business.

Third, there are relatively generous rewards and fringe benefits. A recent survey of high-performing service companies in the US found that they each 'have some of the most liberal and complete programs of fringe benefits in their respective industries. When possible these companies pay wages that exceed union scale . . . nearly all the companies encourage broad stock ownership by employees in addition to their participation in profit-sharing programs' (Heskett, 1986, p. 129). A similar pattern can be seen in Europe, with companies such as Domus and ICA (in Sweden) and Marks and Spencer explicitly keeping their pay levels in the upper quartile for the industry and supporting these with a wide range of other material benefits. These include the frequently neglected but clearly important 'hygiene' factors such as the provision of canteens, restrooms, working uniforms, supporting healthcare services and so on.

Fourth, high levels of involvement and commitment may be sustained by offering all employees – even those in the operating core – the possibility of job moves within the organisation which may increase skills and responsibilities as well as pay. United Parcel Service, for example, offers its drivers the opportunity to become supervisors of other routes and drivers. The position brings with it the opportunity to purchase company stock and for further promotion into management. Marriott Corporation, the US hotel chain, offers non-supervisory employees the chance to participate in the design of their own 90-day training programme to enable movement into higher-paid jobs (Heskett, 1986, pp. 124–5).

Finally, human resource policies oriented to the generation of high employee commitment are characterised by the recognition of achievements in ways which are designed to advertise and therefore reinforce acceptable codes of behaviour. Company newsletters, for example, may cite employees who have excelled in customer service. McDonald's run a competition for the best hamburger maker, which culminates in an All-American contest where, recalls one employee, 'there was a big trophy involved, and I think there was money involved . . . .The important thing was that you got to wear an All-American patch on your shirt' (Peters and Waterman, 1982, p. 258). Such forms of hoopla and razzle-dazzle are frequently reported in the voluminous literature on 'excellent' western corporations – and there are parallel forms of emotive recognition in many Japanese corporations. But perhaps the most powerful form of reinforcement is provided by the role models offered by senior managers of consumer service corporations. Executives who interact within the operating core not only demonstrate 'the right way' to do things but they may also communicate an enthusiasm for the business and a detailed interest in day-to-day operational tasks. In this way, they attempt to encourage the psychological involvement of junior employees. Corporations which attempt to encourage the internationalisation of work standards through such management styles often also develop associated 'family' cultures. But as we know, families differ. Some are egalitarian, flexible and relatively loose; others are paternalistic, hierarchical and disciplined. In general, it would appear that the latter predominate amongst consumer service corporations. This may well reflect the values of their entrepreneur-founders and the preferences of most employees, as well as the technological imperatives of large-scale consumer service provision.

Many of these points are illustrated in the case of ServiceMaster, one of the most successful service businesses in the United States.

ServiceMaster

ServiceMaster provides housekeeping services – maintenance, laundry, linen, food service management, materials management, etc. – to health, commercial and industrial organisations. It has operating revenues of $2 billion and is frequently ranked with the best of large corporations in terms of return on equity. High levels of performance are sustained by meticulous organisation – "the company devotes considerable research to finding the best way of doing a job, often creating its own tools and materials, and ensures that employees are thoroughly trained, and motivated to achieve excellent results" (Morgan, 1989, p. 169). ServiceMaster Chairman Kenneth T Wessner explains the company's achievements in the following terms.

How does a growing service business set management controls that will keep pace with business without threatening to extinguish the organization's entrepreneurial enthusiasm or commitment to personal service for each customer?

It may be argued that services cannot be treated like manufactured goods or that people who provide services cannot be managed with the same system of tight controls as production workers. On the other hand, one cannot expect to endure growth without some kind of accountability system. You may be able to achieve growth, as some companies have, by tapping into the rapidly expanding services market. But the question then becomes one of whether or not you will survive the growth you experienced.

The ultimate responsibility of management is survival, hence the dilemma for a growing service business.

- If you set rigid controls on the expanding delivery system, they may alter the atmosphere , the "package" surrounding the service "product", so that the product no longer is attractive to customers – or to the new employees required to make the expanding system work.
- If you pay little attention to controls, you may see the delivery of service becomes unprofitable or increasingly unwieldy and unreliable.

131

The solution to this dilemma lies in the interaction of two managerial elements: vision and control.

Vision determines why an organization is doing what it is doing. Controls determine how, when, where, with what, and through whom the enterprise is to accomplish its objectives. Successful management depends not simply on establishing these two elements, but on relating them in a way that each has an influence on shaping the other.

This interaction is especially important in a service organization. Unlike customers of a manufacturing concern, which competes on the basis of product comparison, the customer for a service most often will distinguish one provider from another on the basis of their differing management policies. From the customer's point of view, these management policies are seen in the way a service company understands and services their needs.

In the health-care industry, for example, there is a great deal of emphasis currently on cost containment. But the deeper concern of most people in this field – whether administrators or medical professionals – is the quality of care provided the patient. The orientation of people in the health-care professions continues to be primarily one of compassion, of concern for people and caring for their needs.

A service organization that approaches this market with a cost-effective program, but no credible atmosphere of concern for people, will almost certainly provide a negative response. It will have failed to project to customers a feeling that it is aware of what really motivates people in this field, how they perceive the work they are doing, what kind of help they feel they need in doing it.

In the excitement of rapid expansion, it is easy to confer the mantle of a vision in continued growth itself. On the surface, at least, a chorus of "We want to grow!" may seem to ring with enthusiasm. But is commitment to your own growth really visionary? Does it really project a commitment to the customer? Does it portray any sense of social responsibility beyond the narrow aim of making a profit? As attractive as this may be to prospective investors and career-minded employees, how attractive will this essentially self-centred theme appear to those who, by taking on your service, become dependent upon you? Or to those who are critics of free enterprise and advocate its close regulation – or elimination?

The customer and the community at large are concerned with their own needs, not yours. The vision of your company must promise a benefit to them in order to be meaningful to them. But it must do so in a way that is credible. It must indicate an awareness of the realities of business. "We'll do whatever it takes to please you" is not a vision, for example. It is advertising. As your customer knows, effort always implies costs. If you promise to spare no effort, therefore, who is to assume the cost? Will it appear in the price to the customer, in the profit to shareholders, in the pay to your employees, or in some residual social or environmental "cost" charged to the community around you? These are the business realities that must be reflected in your vision.

In my own organization, ServiceMaster Industries Inc., we feel that our corporate purpose – the why of our enterprise – is, in the broadest sense, to have an influence for good in our society, in our government, and in people's lives. To express this in words that are both visionary and realistic we have established four corporate objectives:

1. To honor God in all we do.
2. To help people develop.
3. To pursue excellence.
4. To grow profitably.

By working to accomplish these objectives, we feel we can exercise our responsibilities both externally, to our customers and the community around us, and internally, to our employees and shareholders. Our customers, as well as our employees and shareholders, will agree that it is essential to be profitable if we are to provide the services we have promised to deliver, the career opportunities for employees, and the return on investment made in our company.

We perceive profitable growth not as an end in itself, but as a means through which to achieve other, more visionary objectives. The pursuit of excellence, our third objective, is similarly viewed as a means to an end rather than an end in itself. Our first two objectives – to honor God and to help other people develop – are indeed visionary. But they also are pragmatic in that we recognize how completely they depend on the company's profitable growth and sound management in order to be accomplished.

To be meaningful, vision cannot simply be talked about. It must be lived. It must be made an integral part of the enterprise. It must be incorporated into the lives – both professional and personal – of people throughout the organization. This is where sound management controls play their part.

Controls in a business organization have been defined as a formal system for:

● Establishing objectives
● Measuring and evaluating performance
● Taking action to improve performance

Another definition is that controls are a means of assuring that resources are obtained and used effectively to accomplish the organization's objectives.

Although these definitions have a utilitarian ring to them, they also emphasize the relentless and regulatory nature of controls. Like the governor on an engine, they seem intent on restraining the organization, rather than letting it "rev up" freely. Such definitions do not show much of the spirit of an enterprise that wants to build on a vision and grow at a substantial pace. Remember that the challenge is to find ways for visions and controls to influence each other. Where is the vision in these definitions?

To infuse controls with a vision we need to redefine what they are. Instead of emphasizing the regulatory process, let us speak of the process of building a team, the process of creating a sense of shared enterprise. Controls are not something to be legislated by top management. Instead they should be an expression of top management's leadership. The responsibility of management is not to get employees to toe the line or follow procedures, but rather to help them share in the vision of the company.

How can this be accomplished? One of the most important and effective control mechanisms for building teamwork is education and training. At ServiceMaster, for example, we invest a great deal of time and effort in education and training of people at every level of our company. The focus of this activity is not so much on what we want our people to do, but rather on what we want people to be.

Another essential element of team building for management control is planning. To build teamwork through planning the company must involve employees in determining both the future of the organization and what their own individual role is achieving in that future.

Our current planning process in ServiceMaster looks forward over the next 20 years. There are hundreds of people participating in this process. They represent every segment of the company and every level of management. The effect of this enlarged planning process is a sense of teamwork, a shared interest pervading our plans for the future.

Studies of the impact management controls have on a worker's quality of performance and level of job satisfaction show that three factors are involved in a successful control system:

First, controls must seek to make clear what the organization expects of the individual worker. Second, controls must be established in such a way that the workers feel some sense of influence and control over their work situation. Third, controls must include a formal and continuous evaluation in which the worker can expect rewards for good performance as well as corrective action for failure to meet expectations.

It would be a mistake to focus only on the negative, legislative aspects of this control process. It is counterproductive to stress only the expectations placed on the worker and the promise of corrective action for failure to meet those expectations. Yet this may be the implication most often drawn when the term "controls" is used.

What studies have pointed out consistently is that top performers are motivated by the positive aspects of the control process. Promise of reward is especially important as a motivating factor. But the degree of autonomy a person feels in deciding how to accomplish what is needed by the organization also plays a significant role in motivating top performance. People are motivated to the extent they feel valued as members of the team, able to contribute creatively to achieving the vision.

Further, people are motivated to the extent to which their personal vision corresponds with that of the organization. This dynamic union of purposes between the individual and the organization cannot be legislated. People must be *led* to see the advantages of linking their personal goals with those of the company. How can such leadership be achieved? How does a manager begin to build a team?

The key lies in the effort of the leader to maintain personal and corporate integrity. As part of the initial process of establishing controls, it is necessary that you as a leader:

- Understand yourself. Know what your own values are and what purpose you see for your life.
- Understand your company, the requirements placed on you by its sense of values and purpose.
- Make sure these two elements are compatible.

Out of that compatibility will come a shared sense of vision and purpose that you as a leader can successfully communicate to your workers. You must share the dream. Your personal enthusiasm will attract others to join you in an exciting venture. It also will influence the way your employees respond to the controls you establish. Your personal dedication to accomplishing the vision of your company will be the basis on which your employees judge the fairness of your controls.

That dedication will not be simply to a job. If you are sincere in determining what you stand for, the dedication will become a way of life. The controls you will establish, in that case, will be no more and no less than the disciplines you have imposed on yourself in order to accomplish this vision. Rather than chafe under such controls, your employees will recognize these disciplines as a formula for achieving a level of success and self-realization similar to your own.

Source: Wessner (1981)

ORGANISATIONAL ISSUES

Whatever the precise nature of the corporate culture, large-scale consumer service corporations share a common dilemma. Under considerable financial pressures to sustain growth, they face the threat that greater scale will demand more systems, standards and controls. On the one hand, as we pointed out at the beginning of this chapter, this process of bureaucratisation may damage the delivery of a personal service; on the other, it can become increasingly difficult to nurture or sustain employee flexibility, involvement and innovation. Solutions to this dilemma vary and they involve different trade-offs. In the next chapter we explore the rather different challenges faced by those organisations engaged in the large-scale provision of professional services.

7

TRANSITIONS IN THE PROFESSIONAL SERVICE ORGANISATION

Within all the advanced economies there are well-established professional groups – in medicine, law and education, for example – whose origins actually precede the earliest stages of industrialisation. But the growth of professional occupations, and their location within large-scale organisations, are relatively recent phenomena. The post-war period has seen the emergence of the knowledge-based 'information society' and the associated growth of large professional corporations. As a result, the majority of employment in economies such as the USA and the UK is information-based and the largest single occupational group is professionals. The older professions – law, accountancy, medicine, architecture, accounting, engineering, banking and so on – have been joined by more recent arrivals in design, advertising, consulting, communication/broadcasting and computing. In the process, the typical professional has become an expert salaried employee. As we discussed in Chapter 2, an increasing number work within small-scale professional enterprises which have spun off as a result of the fragmentation of larger corporations. Others are employed within the technostructure or support staff of manufacturing, administrative or consumer service organisations. But many work together in relatively large numbers within the operating core of giant professional service organisations. In the European public sector, these organisations owe their scale to the universal state provision of services in areas such as education and health. In the private sector, scale has been achieved largely by a mixture of rapid organic growth combined with acquisitions and mergers. The pace of this consolidation in sectors such as accounting, consulting and advertising accelerated dramatically during the 1980s.

But whether in public or private hands, the organisational challenge facing large-scale professional enterprises remains the same: the regular, mass production of standardised services via the co-ordination of relatively complex work-tasks. Indeed, it is the complexity of work within the operating core – and its resistance to procedural controls, output measures or tight supervisory monitoring – which distinguishes these from other large-scale organisations discussed in previous chapters. Standardisation of service must be combined with professional autonomy and extensive decentralisation. In a sense, professional organisations can never be more than loosely integrated in structural and cultural terms; attempts to import managerial approaches from elsewhere seem destined to fail.

The culture of consent

Intelligent people prefer to agree rather than to obey.

In despair at the way its programmes were organized, the Business School in one university recruited as the Director of Programmes a successful businessman, who had made a modest fortune in his own business and wanted to move on to a new career. 'I will soon put some order into this place,' he thought, and said. He wrote memoranda to the academics laying down new procedures. No one read the memoranda. He called a meeting. No one came. In frustration, he asked for an explanation.

'These are independent individuals,' he was told, 'you cannot command them to come to a meeting at your convenience; you have to negotiate a time and place convenient to all of them; you had better send round a list with possible alternatives.' He did and they came, or most of them. He explained the new procedures which, he said, would be introduced next month. At that point one of the older faculty members said, gently, 'Bill, in this kind of institution you cannot *tell* us to do anything, you can only *ask* us and try to persuade us to agree'.

'Well then,' Bill said, 'let me ask you what you think we should do to put some sense into this place.'

'No, Bill,' the elder replied, 'that's what we hired *you* for, to come up with those sort of ideas. But they will only work if we agree with them. If we don't, why then you will have to persuade us or come up with some better ideas. This is, you see, an organization of consent, not of command.'

It is, however, not just because they are intelligent individuals that they cannot be commanded. There is often no one to command them. The new organization, as we have seen, will be a flat organization. Like universities they will often have no more than four layers of executives in any operation. People and groups will have . . . big areas of discretion. They will be judged increasingly by results not by the methods which they use. Everyone will have their own psychological territory or organizational space, territory which is theirs and which cannot be entered on without permission.

Source: Handy (1990, pp. 128–9)

'Cultures of consent' are effective where conscientious and capable professionals share a commitment to common, client-centred goals and trust each other. Lengthy, intensive training and socialisation as well as organisational relations which facilitate rather than hinder the effective deployment of professional knowledge are critical influences. Under such circumstances, professionals are more likely to use their autonomy responsibly, in ways which benefit consumers and do not undermine colleagues. Organisational performance, professional development and client interests are thus in harmony. But professionals are *not* always equally capable; to believe this is to accept at face value the professionals' own ideology. Nor do they uniformly share the same level of conscientiousness in relation to their clients or colleagues; some appear to put self-interest above all else. Finally, the organisational deployment of professionals is frequently less than optimum. Shortcomings such as these are at the root of many managerial problems within professional service organisations. The conventional guardians of standards have been, of course, the professionals themselves, via strategies of credential-based occupational selectivity. But the rigorous concern with standards in the 'gatekeeping function' is sometimes less evident once professional status is achieved. In the absence of collegial control, professional employees typically prove highly resistant to any attempts at 'external' management.

Managing professional service organisations: key problems

1   Influencing standards amongst those who effectively train themselves.
2   Coping with poor performance when professionals have tenure.

3 Developing managerial and administrative skills amongst those regarding such work as unimportant.

4 Encouraging organisational involvement when professional careers demand mobility.

5 Co-ordinating individuals who enjoy high levels of autonomy.

6 Exercising control within informal loose structures.

7 Determining duties and responsibilities through processes of mutual adjustment.

8 Nurturing collective identification amongst individualistic professionals.

Difficulties such as these have not prevented attempts, during the 1980s and 1990s, to restructure organisations in ways which might allow greater control over professional employees. Initiatives have been taken across a broad front. In universities, academic tenure has been replaced by fixed-term contracts; in hospitals, doctors report to 'professional managers' and prescribe drugs from approved lists; in accountancy firms, consultants complete personal time sheets. In the public sector, these managerial changes have coincided with a fundamental re-examination of organisational mission. Traditional notions of 'public service' which were powerful sources of recruitment, integration and commitment in health, education and public sector broadcasting, for example, have been undermined but not as yet, critics would claim, replaced by any new sense of shared purpose. The debate is shaped, of course, by wider socio-economic and political influences, which have led to a questioning of collective public provision (for example, in national health care provision and public broadcasting corporations) as well as collective – and sometimes exclusionary – private professional organisations (for example, those representing medics and lawyers). In their place, attempts have been made to strengthen market relations and individual consumer preferences. Such changes have been described as amongst 'the most dramatic management shifts of modern times' (Caulkin, 1994). But whether defending the status quo or arguing for change, discussions are inevitably muddied by the sheer difficulties of accurately assessing the organisational performance of public sector professional service organisations. How, for example, is the effectiveness of the British Broadcasting Corporation to be judged? Janet Morgan, when Special Advisor to the Director General, made the following observations.

The issues she raises continue to be a focus for public debate in the mid-1990s.

Measuring performance in public service

Professional organisations

Organisations do have lives. They do go through phases and the BBC is no exception. It is suffering from the sclerosis that tends eventually to affect all institutions and organisations. After some sixty years this is not surprising . . . .

The BBC is a very good example of a bureaucratic organisation. Its affairs are run in carefully delegated ways, each level of the hierarchy, from the top of the pyramid to the wide layers at the bottom, having its own degree of discretion in decision-making. There is a very definite hierarchy and, the further up you go, the more mystique each superior level enjoys. The BBC shares the defensiveness of all bureaucratic organisations, with the appropriate secretiveness, too. That secretiveness and mystery is protected and enhanced by the use of jargon, in particular the use of initials, to baffle the outsider. There is much emphasis on team spirit and the whole operation is infused with an interesting mixture of arrogance and panic, plus a degree of paranoia. . . .

In the commercial world it is easier to tell when something is, if not dead, moribund, because the state of the balance sheet shows when life is draining away. With an organisation like the BBC, however, you can never be quite sure when brain death has actually occurred. There we have no balance sheet, no simple criteria of success or failure. Producers and managers, like all human beings, search endlessly for ways of measuring how well they are doing. The ratings are little use; the test is much more in whether or not there is a general feeling of success, of esteem. The BBC is not the only organisation whose members depend on such woolly tests. The National Health Service, the universities – all such organisations have similar problems with trying to measure how well they are doing. In any case, for all the government's efforts to draw up criteria based on social transfers and such like, how do we know what is meant by 'doing well'? The assessment of success is to a large extent not measurable. That is the reason why it is hard to tell how lively – or not – the BBC actually remains.

Source: Morgan (1986, pp. 22–4)

ORGANISATIONAL STRUCTURE AND MANAGEMENT STYLE

In one sense, the organisational problems of professional service corporations are those earlier referred to as 'new entrepreneurial enterprises' writ large. In both circumstances, work processes are organised around relationships amongst professional experts and between them and their clients. Similarly, there are dangers that excessively strong external orientations can lead to staff regarding their employing organisations as little more than a resource base enabling them to meet personal client requirements and develop their own professional reputation. Indeed, free from the careful eye of an active owner-manager, the opportunities for professional abuse and the risks of organisational fragmentation may, in some circumstances, be even greater.

However, there are important differences between smaller and larger forms of professional organisation. First, as a result of scale – and sometimes technology – the corporate professional may be removed from either direct or lengthy interactions with clients. Pressures to process larger numbers may, in effect, distance professionals from their clients, as with the overworked junior doctor in a large hospital, or the professor with too many classes. In these circumstances, it is unlikely that individual clients will feel able to direct or control the activities of professional providers. Second, large-scale professional organisations will normally have grown a managerial middle line although, admittedly, the hierarchy may be relatively flat and with limited power. It may also be staffed with ex-professionals whose managerial abilities are limited. Nevertheless, its existence serves to separate the strategic apex from the operating core and, more generally, impacts upon the nature of organisational relationships. Third, larger professional organisations will have developed, to varying degrees of sophistication, a technostructure responsible for the production of, for example, work standards, operating procedures, reward systems and so on. Over recent years the power of some technostructures has been reinforced by state-initiated attempts to exercise greater control over public sector professionals. Again, health, education and broadcasting services are good examples in countries such as the UK, Canada, Australia and France. The success of such strategies is often dependent upon the extent to which technostructures can be staffed by 'outsiders' rather than 'infiltrated' by professionals from the operating core. In the UK, the dissolution of the University Grants Committee and its replacement by the Higher Education Funding Council is an interesting recent example of the partial substitution of the latter by the former. Finally, scale impacts upon the nature of relationships within the operating core. In the absence of special projects, programmes or other team-based activities, relationships between professional colleagues (even within specialist departments) can become fleeting and depersonalised. The division of labour between professionals and others can be subject to renegotiation, particularly under pressure of work overload. This pattern has been sensitively explored by one observer in the United States.

Divisions of labour in the professional operating core

Within an organization the situation is quite different. . . . The standard interprofessional division of labour is replaced by the interorganizational one. More often than not, this locates professionals where they must assume many extraprofessional tasks and cede many professional ones. To be sure, the organizational division of labour may be formalized in job descriptions that recognize professional boundaries, but these have a rather vague relation to reality. In most professional work settings, actual divisions of labour are established, through negotiation and custom, that embody situation-specific rules of professional jurisdiction. These actual divisions of labour exist over relatively short time periods – perhaps a few months to a couple of years. They are extremely vulnerable to organizational perturbations. Professional staff are often replaced by paraprofessional or untrained staff without corresponding change of function. The division of labour must then be renegotiated, with the common result that boundaries of actual professional jurisdiction change to accommodate organizational imperatives.

It is in the workplaces, then, that the actual complexity of professional life insists on having its effect. Here, for example, the diversity within professions must be recognized. If a professional is incompetent, organizational function demands that his or her work be done by someone else who is probably not officially qualified to do it. Or if there is too much professional work, nonprofessionals do it. Boundaries between professional jurisdictions therefore tend to disappear in worksites, particularly in overworked worksites. There results a form of knowledge transfer that can be called workplace assimilation. Subordinate professionals, nonprofessionals, and members of related, equal professions learn on the job a craft version of given professions' knowledge systems. While they lack the theoretical training that justifies membership in that profession, they generally acquire much of the diagnostic, therapeutic, and inferential systems . . . .This assimilation is facilitated by the fact that professionals are not in reality a homogeneous group. In the jurisdictional system of the workplace, it is the real output of an individual, not his credentialed or noncredentialed status, that matters. Since some professionals are much more talented than others, the best of the subordinates often excel the worst of the superordinates; certain individuals in closely related professions end up knowing far more about a profession's actual work than do a fair number of its own practitioners.

The reality of jurisdictional relations in the workplace is therefore a fuzzy reality indeed. To be sure, in the elite workplaces – the university teaching hospitals, the Wall Street law firms, the leading architectural houses – the blurring is minimized. Since each group is represented by its best members, vertical and horizontal assimilation can be minimized. (On occasion it is encouraged on the grounds of facilitating organizational function, even in elite firms; the great architectural firms are examples.) But in most professional worksites, the mix of workers is so broad that assimilation is considerable. It reaches its maximum in publicly funded worksites specializing in pariah clients – mental hospitals, jails, criminal courts – where few elite professionals venture, and where attendants, guards, and clerks effectively conduct such professional work as is done.

Source: Abbott (1988, pp. 65–66)

Abbott's analysis shows that although strict controls may be applied to the achievement of professional status, the day-to-day division of labour in the work-place is unlikely to correspond strictly with individual actors' acquisition of formal credentials. Thus, the work of conveyancing is performed by administrative assistants rather than solicitors; teaching and assessment is undertaken by partially qualified research associates rather than full professors; and medications are administered by attendants rather than doctors. The consequences of such practices may vary. Those formally unqualified staff who find themselves, unexpectedly perhaps, undertaking the work of professionals may feel their jobs have been 'enriched'. For others, this kind of on-the-job exposure may represent the early stages of their own transition to professional status. But in the absence of such opportunities, other staff may simply feel exploited; carrying the responsibilities of professional work but without the attendant status or material rewards. In some cases, as with house conveyancing in the USA and UK, the domain of professional work may eventually be redefined through state legislation. Elsewhere, the formal recognition of new workplace responsibilities may be accelerated by the application of new technology. The shifting of some medical diagnosis work in hospitals from doctors to technicians is a recent example. Renegotiating the division of labour can, then, become the focus of considerable conflict within the operating core of large professional organisations.

Although, then, large-scale professional organisations have certain features in common, they may also differ from each other in many respects. Benveniste (1987) distinguishes four models with distinctive structures and managerial approaches.

Professional organisations: a typology

1 Partnership model

Self-selected professional group manages the organisation.

Examples

Law, accountancy, management consulting.

Characteristics

- Professional content of work central to organisation mission.
- Specialised by professionalism or client/market.
- Size beneficial but low levels of internal integration.
- Equity participation an important motivator of individual and group performance.

Strengths

- Professional control.
- Clear professional career path to top.
- Senior professional role models.

Weaknesses

- Partnership opportunities limited.
- Excellent professionals may make mediocre managers.
- Partner conflicts difficult to resolve.

---

2 Senior staff model

Single manager shares responsibility with selected senior professionals.

Examples

Media, research and development, social service agencies, voluntary associations.

Characteristics

- Professional knowledge (experience important to managerial decision-making).
- Professional autonomy important source of motivation.
- Centralisation requirements higher than professional model.

Strengths

- Clearer managerial responsibility at the top.
- Combined with professional inputs and participation.
- Differentiated career ladder combining managerial and professional roles.

Weaknesses

- Authority conflicts between senior professional and managerial staff.
- Excessive intervention by top manager.

3 Dual governance model

Two hierarchies: some managerial responsibilities vested in a professional body; others allocated to administration.

Examples

Universities, hospitals.

Characteristics

- Professional participation in selected management decisions crucial.
- Professional participation important motivator.
- Some managerial tasks do not require professional inputs.
- Professional consensus is important.
- Stable environment facilitates careful assessment of professional choices.

Strengths

- Participation institutionalised.
- Decision-making by consensus.

Weaknesses

- Professional v. administrator conflict institutionalised.
- Slow, cumbersome decision-making processes.

4 Collegial model

All managerial responsibilities vested in entire professional membership.

Examples

Voluntary organisations, pressure groups

Characteristics

- Small-scale.
- Complex tasks.

147

- High-trust relations.
- Commitment to 'ideals'.

Strengths

- Sustains commitment, involvement.
- Adaptive, responsive to environmental shifts.
- Egalitarian, democratic decision processes.

Weaknesses

- Conflicts time-consuming and potentially corrosive.
- No career ladder.
- Instability in long term.

(Source: Benveniste (1987, pp. 85–93)

In both the partnership and senior staff models the strategic apex is dominated by professionals although, in the latter case, a senior managerial role is differentiated. In the dual governance model both the strategic apex and the middle line are split between administrators, on the one hand, and professionals on the other. Finally, in the collegial model, structural divisions between the strategic apex, the middle line and the operating core are, in effect, dissolved.

Set against this context, what kind of changes have occurred within professional organisations over recent years? The remainder of this section reviews three distinct organisational processes which are evident in different types of professional service enterprises: (1) the focus/fragment strategy within senior staff organisations; (2) the strengthening of techocractic controls in partnerships; and (3) the reinforcement of the middle line in dual governance and collegial organisations. In the senior staff model the organisation attempts to build strong professional integration only amongst a reduced and focused core of senior managers, professional and technical staff who constitute full-time 'strategically significant' employees. However, most of the work undertaken within the operating core and by support staff is contracted out to a variety of suppliers, ranging from freelance individuals to large specialist service enterprises. The task of those remaining within the core becomes, in effect, that of formulating product/market strategies and then implementing these through the selection and co-ordination of subcontract suppliers. This model limits the need for an elaborate managerial hierarchy since the work of suppliers is not excessively dependent upon direct supervisory controls. Instead, the critical skills in the core derive from the professional ability to select and develop networks of high-quality providers and to devise rigorous assessments of the outcomes they produce. The greater the extent to which work outputs can be standardised, the less reliance has to be placed upon procedures or supervision. Under these conditions, freelance professionals in the network may experience an enhanced sense of personal autonomy and responsibility, while those within the operating core can concentrate on developing their expert competence.

The emergence of this focus/fragment strategy within media-related professional services was discussed in Chapter 2. In television, publishing and advertising, for example, 'slimmed down' corporations function as commissioning agents for programmes, books and promotions produced by intricate networks of authors, editors, artists and technicians. Indeed, it is this process which accounts for the recent growth of small-scale enterprises in the professional sector. The broader trend towards organisational fragmentation is also apparent in other sectors; indeed, Handy suggests that it may even become apparent within more conventionally structured organisations such as schools.

The shamrock school

At present schools are bedeviled by the need to offer choice to a wide variety of students without running foul of the bureaucracy and anonymity that is inevitable in a large organization. . . .

The alternative is to think upside-down and turn the school into a shamrock with a core activity and everything else contracted out or done part-time by a flexible labour force. The core activity would be primarily one of educational manager, devising an appropriate educational programme for each child and arranging for its delivery. A core curriculum would continue to be taught directly by the school but anything outside the core would be contracted out to independent suppliers, new mini-schools. There might then be a range of independent art schools, language schools, computing schools, design schools and others. These independent suppliers would be paid, by the core school, on a per capita basis, probably with an agreed minimum.

The job of the school proper would be to set and monitor the standards of these mini-school outsiders, to ensure an adequate variety, to help students and their families decide on an educational programme from all that was available and to manage a core curriculum itself in order to maintain some sense of group cohesion at the centre.

In this way the school as a whole could be quite big because for most of the time the students would be in smaller mini-schools. The parents would choose, not so much between schools as within schools, between the variety that was on offer. In big schools there could be a number of competing outside institutions offering courses in one particular area, such as art or languages.

Source: Handy (1990, pp. 169–79)

A second organisational strategy rests upon the application of strong technocratic controls. This method of integration has been most extensively applied within the global partnership professional enterprises which have emerged over the last ten years in areas such as accounting, management consulting and advertising. In these firms opportunities to subcontract have been limited by the need to retain control over in-house recipes which become, in effect, intellectual capital and as such major sources of competitive advantage. On the other hand, the traditional mechanism for professional integration – equity-based partnership – breaks down in the face of increasing numbers. As a result, auditors, consultants and account executives find themselves more closely controlled by procedural measures, time-log analyses and fee income targets. Such organisations are co-ordinated, therefore, by a mixture of professional and technical controls; the middle line remains flat and under-elaborated, with real managerial power concentrated in the equity partners dominating the strategic apex. The long-term viability of these organisational forms is questionable. There are powerful internal forces for disintegration, reflected in the spectacular decline in the 1990s of many partnerships which had grown rapidly during the growth period of the previous decade. Even the more stable professional businesses face considerable human resource challenges if they are to retain the commitment of large numbers of highly skilled, potentially mobile staff who have limited opportunity to acquire partnership status.

The third organisational strategy, most evident within the dual governance model, is through strengthening of the middle line. In the public services this has been triggered primarily by a crisis of resources. In the health services, for example, attempts to reduce costs within the operating core have often been driven by hospital line managers. In effect, power has been decentralised from state departments and regional health authorities and delegated into highly autonomous operating centres. The middle line itself has, in turn, been strengthened – in relation to the operating core – by the recruitment of specialist, non-medical administrators. In efforts to establish their position, this new cadre of 'professional managers' typically create technostructures through the implementation of various operational and financial control mechanisms. At the same time, in the interests of flexibility and cost reduction, the support services – catering, cleaning, security and so on – are subcontracted out to private suppliers. Changes which began in the middle line, then, have reverberated within all aspects of hospital organisations. The emergence of non-medical managers has often created predictable operational clashes with medical professionals. In addition, the combination of pressures resulting from large-scale organisational change and cost reduction measures seems to have overloaded many front-line professionals within the operating core and led to the depersonalisation of the professional–client relationship.

STAFFING PROFESSIONAL SERVICE ORGANISATIONS: EMPLOYEES AND THEIR REWARDS

Clearly, changes in the structure and management of professional service organisations have major implications for the jobs of those employed within them. Individual experience will vary, of course, according to which organisational strategies are pursued and where employees are located within the structure – operating core, line management, support staff and so on. Many of the changes discussed in this chapter have undoubtedly made some kinds of professional employment less attractive. The autonomy, status and privileges conventionally associated with professional qualification have been gradually eroded in large organisations by a variety of administrative and technocratic controls. Resource cut-backs and related attempts to reduce cost have led, in some cases, to dramatic examples of work overload. When such changes are combined with a wider questioning of the 'contribution' made by professionals – as, for example, with those in teaching and medical occupations over recent years – then the retention of existing staff as well as the future supply of new entrants is threatened. These points are graphically illustrated by the inside view provided below by one hospital doctor. The declining attractiveness of professional employment has sometimes led to the wholesale recruitment of qualified staff from other countries.

Slaves to the hospital bleep

The House year is a nightmare. Working 80–120 hours in a week defies adequate description. The longest continuous stretch most of us do is 80 hours. This means starting work at 8am on Friday and finishing at 5pm on Monday. During this time you are on call constantly and you could be awake for every minute. At the end you are allowed to go home provided that your patients are all sorted out. If not, you may have to stay until 6.00 or 7.00 or 8.00. But, remember, you must be awake and alert at 8am Tuesday. There are no days off after nights on call.

The mood swings that accompany such shifts are almost pathological. You become convinced that other hospital staff are plotting to make life even worse than it appears. The warm working relationship with nurses, radiographers and laboratory staff that was eagerly built in the first few days is soon in tatters. Quiet annoyance explodes into anger. This is usually taken out on pillows or cushions away from patients. But it is not uncommonly taken out on nursing staff who happen to be in the wrong place at the wrong time. The system is despised. Junior doctors feel hopeless and helpless; they are small fish in an unknown sea. Chronic sleeplessness causes utter exhaustion and occasionally breakdown. We are trapped. The system is utterly inflexible.

The shift starts with accepting GPs' requests to admit their patients. In some hospitals this can involve time spent trying to find an empty bed, searching floor by floor and ward by ward. Nurses are often primed to inform you that their beds are blocked, ready for routine admissions the next day.

When patients arrive they need to get undressed, be put into bed and have their blood pressure, pulse and temperature recorded. All this is generally accepted as a nurse's job, but all too often the over-worked nurses don't have time. Often the junior doctor arrives to find the patient still bundled up in the chair by the bed.

Once they are in bed, our five years of training comes into its own. We ask the patient what is wrong, what they've had done in the past, what pills they take before we dive into the all-rewarding and all-revealing examination. Given time to write all this out, the doctor then has a rare opportunity to consider what may be wrong with the patient, how to prove his hypothesis and then what to do about it.

The proving can involve blood tests, putting up a drip, prescribing drugs (and giving them immediate intravenous ones if these are required), recording an ECG, arranging X-rays and more. Each test requires at least one phone call and can take anything from two minutes to two hours to arrange depending on the presence of laboratory staff, the telephone line being free, and freedom from interruption by the bleep with news of new admissions or problems elsewhere.

Once preliminary results are back (or earlier), the registrar can be informed. His review of the patient creates further work, more tests, different treatment. If the registrar has the time and inclination he may actually teach you on the case or he may just order you to carry out his plan of management.

If we all had only a handful of patients the house officer could do everything. On average, I guess, most of us have about 20 patients, though sometimes we can have 40 or more. This method of admitting a patient takes about 30–60 minutes. There's no time to allay patients' fears or even to explain what is going on.

The most despised object is the bleep. It constantly interrupts a day's work. Introduced to improve efficiency, it now does the opposite. We often get calls from those who believe that if we are not working in front of their very eyes we are lazing around in the doctors' mess. The problem is rarely urgent and often could have waited until we were next on the ward. However, the bleep is seen as a quick fix, and no regard is paid to the disruption it causes. The immediacy and ease of the bleep system have led to its excessive use. It is not unknown to stand by a phone doing nothing but answer bleep after bleep: no sooner have you dealt with one than another ear-piercingly announces itself. No activities are immune. The bleep intrudes on new patients, distracts you from telephone conversations, and disrupts those delicate sessions when you are breaking bad news. The result is that bleep calls, unless obviously important, are dealt with abruptly and aggressively. In the name of efficiency we degrade, humiliate, patronise and shout. It's a sad state of affairs and not a good way for professionals to communicate.

The time allowed for us to recall our undergraduate knowledge and apply it to the clinical situation is never enough. Instead of trying to understand an illness, its investigation and management we are forced to run a barrage of routine tests to cover every possible diagnosis, to provide every tiny detail regardless of how useful it really is. This has little benefit for the patient or the hospital budget. It also means that doctors arrange tests ad nauseam but do not think about their patients' problems and rarely get a detailed history (which, as undergraduates, we were taught was 90 per cent of the problem-solving technique).

It is not just our own workload which prevents us learning; our seniors too are often in such a rush to get around all the patients they have little time to teach the juniors; and so the feedback which could provide so much just isn't there. Apart form the large numbers of patients that we all look after, our workload is increasingly being taken up by procedures which provide no useful experience.

Most professions complain about paperwork, but hospital notes are appalling and in a system undergoing a financial squeeze no one person exists to maintain patients' notes. Too often it falls to the junior doctor to spend hours searching old temperature and drug charts for useful notes. If blood test or X-ray results cannot be found easily it is quicker to repeat them. This epitomises a hospital's inefficiency. Because of financial cutbacks, in many hospitals it has formally become the junior's job to file the results, but often they are in such a mess that the whole lot needs to be rehoused and sorted out. This can take hours. Five years of training to file paperwork. What a waste.

It is a myth that junior doctors are well paid. We only appear well paid because we work so many hours. But look at the figures: during each eight-hour day, 40 hour week we earn about £6 an hour. For every hour after this we earn about £2.20 – just over one third of the normal rate, not time and a third. At this hourly rate we are probably cheaper than the cleaners, cheaper than the porters. Yet we are responsible for ill people's lives.

Most of us have been aiming for a medical career for six or more years. By the end of the house year it is inconceivable to think of getting out even though the work of a senior house officer is often little better. This sinking ship needs all hands on deck. Our desire to help ill people still burns strong but we need recognition of our abilities and release from inappropriate duties.

The system, and ultimately the patients, are losing out.

Source: The Guardian, 25 September, 1991

An alleged devaluation of status amongst some professional groups –
particularly public sector employees – could be undermining morale
and thereby generating a more instrumental orientation to work and
hence a redefinition of the psychological contract. At the same time
a number of professional occupations have become 'feminised'
which, claim some observers, is an index of devalued status, diminished rewards and limited career opportunities. The trends, however,
are not entirely consistent; they may apply to women in teaching, for
example, but less to those in the legal and accounting professions. In
several professions, old and new, women continue to dominate the
junior and middle echelons but are excluded from the strategic apex
(Podmore and Spencer, 1987).

But how is the performance of professional employees to be
assessed? This is a key issue driving many of the changes occurring
within public sector organisations. Conventionally, the process has
been managed by professional colleagues according to custom and
practice and collectively agreed criteria. However, managers in the
middle line argue that such an approach is detrimental to the pursuit
of organisational efficiency, and the satisfaction of consumer/client
needs. Accordingly, they are implementing a number of procedures
typical of more bureaucratic organisations and based upon measurable criteria for performance. But what are the appropriate performance indicators and subsequent reward systems for motivating
professional employees? How, for example, should doctors be
assessed; according to patient satisfaction, professional attitude,
effort, cure rate or, perhaps, a combination of all of these? If there
are multiple criteria, how comparable are they and how can short-
and long-term considerations be balanced? Crude attempts to import
the machinery of performance management from corporate contexts
far removed from professional service organisations would appear
inappropriate.

In the long term, professional service organisations also face
choices concerning the career structures offered to their staff. Typically, organisational structures are relatively flat and professionals seek
advancement through their occupational rather than organisational
strategies. In this sense, professionals have always managed their own
careers and expected to be mobile within national and international
labour markets. Unlike managers within administrative organisations,

most professionals are not overdependent on a corporate career within a limited number of organisations. But three problem areas, linked to distinct career stages, are common to many professional service organisations. The first concerns the ambiguous relationship between professional and administrative roles. For some, a move into an administrative role constitutes upward mobility; for others it may represent a rejection of professional ambitions. Which view predominates depends upon the balance between professional and managerial cultures – which clearly varies between different organisations. Nevertheless, in the process, a highly competent professional can become an incompetent – and demotivated – administrator. Twin career tracks are one solution to this familiar dilemma, although the organisational legitimacy of the 'dedicated' administrator is often difficult to establish. A second problem relates to 'professional obsolescence' as the personal knowledge base developed during the early stages of a career becomes outdated. Some professions are more prone to this than others; compare, for example, a constitutional lawyer with a computer scientist. Even in areas where the knowledge base shifts rapidly, older professionals may manage the process by giving greater weight to their mentoring role in relation to junior colleagues. Nevertheless, some professional organisations have significant numbers of staff in mid-career who display symptoms of 'burnout' and whose labour market options are limited. Their very presence exacerbates a third problem: retaining and developing high performers who display exceptional talent and ability early in their careers. Creating organisational opportunities for such professionals is difficult when many, more senior, organisational positions are blocked by older, less able colleagues. In general, it seems that high-performing generalists tend to survive their specialist colleagues. But for both cases the capacity of large-scale organisations to create the conditions which will sustain very high levels of professional performance over long periods of time appears limited.

ORGANISATIONAL ISSUES

In both public and private sectors, large-scale professional service organisations face major managerial challenges. They must provide regular, standardised services to large numbers of customers through

156

the co-ordination of complex work tasks. In the process they are obliged to grant considerable autonomy to staff who are expensive and highly resistant to 'external' attempts to manage them. Control of the 'professional repertoire' remains a critical issue, variously affected by organisational design, external state controls and consumer demands. Professional organisations may be, as some claim, models for the future, but their loosely integrated nature – both amongst professional groups and between them and their support staff – continue to present severe managerial problems. Indeed, it may be that such problems can only be resolved through a transition to the network structures that we discuss in our final chapter.

8

TOWARDS ADHOCRATIC AND NETWORK STRUCTURES

'The kind of organisation which will be operating successfully in the future seems to be one which incorporates either the small business orientation, or the global conglomerate approach, or is the bustling, innovative organisation crammed full of entrepreneurs.'

(Wilson and Rosenfeld, 1990, p. 457)

'Networks are faster, smarter and more flexible than reorganizations or downsizings . . . In effect, a network identifies the 'small company inside the large company' and empowers it to make the four-dimensional trade-offs – among functions, business units, geography and global customers – that determine success in the marketplace.'

(Charan, 1991, p. 104)

As discussed in the opening chapters of this book, dramatic shifts in the business environment during the 1980s and 1990s have accelerated the search for new ways of organisation which facilitate entrepreneurial capabilities. The aim is to combine operational efficiency and cost effectiveness – attributes commonly associated with large-scale organisations – with flexibility, responsiveness, and innovation – characteristics conventionally linked with smaller enterprises. The ideal, it seems, is to achieve global organisation and local responsiveness simultaneously. In the words of Percy Barnevick, chief executive officer of ABB, 'we want to be global and local, big and small, decentralised with centralised reporting' (Bahrami, 1992, p. 33). In attempting to achieve these apparently conflicting goals, many business corporations have drastically reshaped their organisational structures. Centrally managed, vertically integrated corporations

159

fragment into smaller, market-focused business units co-ordinated by several centres not one. Hierarchies are flattened and overlaid with project teams, task forces and other mechanisms of lateral integration. Organisations once operating across several businesses shrink by focusing upon areas of 'core' strength and spinning off, out-sourcing and subcontracting other activities. Each of these changes may be interpreted, at least in part, as organisational strategies designed to initiate and empower 'small business' relations within the context of large, established corporations. Taken together they entail shifts both in intra- and inter-organisational relations. Kanter (1990) refers to these as 'postentrepreneurial' businesses while others point to the emergence of 'contractual structures', 'hollow corporations', 'shamrock' and 'cluster organisations'. For some the changes constitute nothing less than the emergence of the 'post-industrial' corporation.

Post-industrial structures

Lewis Galoob Toys

Lewis Galoob Toys Inc. is obviously a successful company. It sold $58 million worth of its sword-wielding Golden girls "action figures" and other trendy toys last year – 10 times the 1981 total. Yet by traditional standards of structure, strategy, and management practice, Galoob is hardly a company at all.

A mere 115 employees run the entire operation. Independent inventors and entertainment companies dream up most of Galoob's products, while outside specialists do most of the design and engineering. Galoob farms out manufacturing and packaging to a dozen or so contractors in Hong Kong, and they, in turn, pass on the most labour-intensive work to factories in China. When the toys land in the U.S., they're distributed by commissioned manufacturers' representatives. Galoob doesn't even collect its accounts. It sells its receivables to Commercial Credit Corp., a factoring company that also sets Galoob's credit policy. In short, says Executive Vice-President Robert Galoob, "our business is one of relationships." Galoob and his brother, David, the company's president spend their time making all the pieces of the toy company fit together, with their phones, facsimile machines, and telexes working overtime. Galoob is just one of a crowd of companies emerging in toys, garments, electronics, sporting goods, and other industries that are as different from today's industrial giants as early mammals were from dinosaurs. In management jargon, these new corporations are "vertically disaggregated," relying on other companies for manufacturing and many crucial business functions. They are industrial companies without industrial production. And they just may be the organizational model for businesses in the post-industrial era.

Source: Business Week, 3 March, 1986

Benetton

Benetton was a vertically de-integrated company, not only in manufacturing, but also in the three other main activities that constituted its value chain: styling and design, logistics and distribution, and sales. The company relied on external people and companies for the major part of these crucial activities. It employed some 1500 people at the end of 1987.

The styling or design of the garments was done outside the company by a number of international freelance stylists. Giuliana Benetton, with a staff of about 20 people in the product development department, interpreted the 'look' created by the stylists and performed the modelling phase.

More than 80% of manufacturing was done outside the company, by 350 subcontractors employing about 10,000 people. In-house production accounted for the remaining less than 20% (mainly dyeing) and was performed by 700–800 people.

Logistics and distribution activities were also performed mainly by outsiders. For storage the company used a single, huge warehouse for finished products. In addition, the logistics department at Benetton was in charge of delivering the finished garments to the stores all over the world.

Finally, the company utilized an external sales organisation of almost 80 agents to take care of a retailing system of nearly 4000 shops spread all over the world. The internal part of this activity was performed by seven area managers who co-ordinated the selling system as a whole, divided by territories.

Source: Harvard Business School Case 9–389–074, 1988

But although organisations which are built around networks – like Galoob Toys in the US, or Benetton in Europe – may differ from more conventional bureaucratic forms, they are not new. Indeed, the British industrial revolution was constructed around extensive subcontracting networks in industries such as iron and steel, engineering and cotton. The pattern persisted during the twentieth century – in and beyond Britain – in coalmining, shipbuilding and car manufacturing; and 'traditional' networks of one kind or another continue today in sectors such as publishing, clothing, footwear and construction. What *is* new is the increasing application of this organisational form within growth sectors such as telecommunications, computing, consumer electronics and the media industries and its gradual re-adoption, as a result of 'vertical disaggregation', within industries such as transport, engineering and the manufacture of fashion goods.

Many of the central features of these 'network' organisations were anticipated in early theoretical discussions of alternatives to bureaucracy. For example, in the 1960s Burns and Stalker's widely cited analysis of 'organic' structures (1961) was later followed up by others enthusiastically heralding the emergence of 'integrative' (Kanter, 1985) and 'adhocratic' (Toffler, 1985) organisations. The key contrasts between 'mechanistic' and 'organic' structures, as originally outlined, may be briefly summarised as follows.

Context and structure: mechanistic and organic organisations

Environmental factors

Mechanistic	**Organic**
● Simple stable environment.	● Complex dynamic environment.
● Routine processing of standardised materials.	● Non-routine processing of variable materials.
● Large scale.	● Small scale.
● Unskilled operatives.	● Skilled managerial, technical and professional workers.

Organisational types

Mechanistic	**Organic**
● Problems/tasks broken down.	● Problems/tasks not broken down.
● Individual tasks seen as separate from tasks of whole.	● Individual tasks seen in context.

162

- Precise definition of procedures, duties, powers ih each functional area.

- Continual adjustment and and redefinition of roles through interaction with others.

- Hierarchical structure of control and authority.

- Network structure: autonomy, discretion, responsibility according to expertise.

- Vertical interaction and communication (instructions, decisions).

- Lateral interaction and communication (information, consultation and advice)

Mintzberg's (1983) more recent description of the organic form – the 'adhocracy' – depicts an organisation with few traces of formal hierarchy, unable to rely on any form of standardisation for co-ordination; instead, its activities are integrated primarily through processes of mutual adjustment. But whereas within smaller businesses such a process can be expected to occur 'naturally' through informal face-to-face relations, in large corporations it must be facilitated by more formalised mechanisms such as project teams, task forces and matrix structures.

Although 'adhocracies' and 'networks' share certain characteristics, there are also differences. Some insight into these may be captured, following Morgan (1989), by picturing the transition from mechanistic bureaucracies to loosely integrated networks (See Figure 8.1).

Model 1 depicts the classic machine bureaucracy. Work roles are clearly specified and departments rigidly defined. Organisational tasks are co-ordinated through a hierarchical chain of command, with tight central control exercised by the chief executive. This organisation is well adapted to a stable environment, as discussed in earlier chapters. Model 2 emerges when the environment begins to consistently generate new problems which cannot be handled by purely bureaucratic routines. A senior management team is formed and meets on a regular basis to cope with emergent issues. When this team cannot handle all such problems – due to sheer volume as well as the increasing need for cross-functional perspectives – they are supported by project teams and task forces at lower levels, as in Model 3. But departmental loyalties remain strong, and 'real problems' continue to be referred up the hierarchy for a decision. With

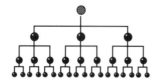

Model 1: The rigid bureaucracy

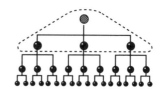

Model 2: The bureaucracy with a senior management team

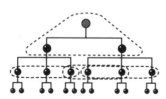

Model 3: The bureaucracy with project teams and task forces

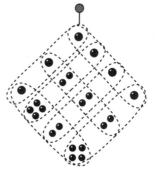

Model 4: The matrix organisation

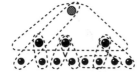

Model 5: The project organisation

Model 6: The loosely-coupled organic network

Figure 8.1 From bureaucracy to network
(Source: Morgan, 1989, p66)

power and, in effect, promotion chances remaining largely within functions, such organisations may appear more flexible than they really are. This may change with the emergence of the Model 4 matrix structure. Equal priority is given to function – for example, marketing, finance, production – and end product or business. Those within the matrix must work with a dual focus and resolve possible conflicts between them rather than through the hierarchy. The aim is to balance professional and functional expertise with customer responsiveness and flexibility. But in practice this equilibrium can be difficult to achieve. Model 5 takes the process a step further; most activities are co-ordinated through relatively autonomous project teams, with functional departments playing only a supporting role. A high premium is placed upon learning, creativity and innovation within and between teams. Interaction and exchange between teams is at a high level, both laterally and vertically, between senior managers and team leaders. Frequent appeals may be made to 'core values' and 'corporate mission' to pull together this loosely integrated structure. Finally, in Model 6 the organic network emerges with a small core at the centre providing strategic direction and support while operational activities are subcontracted to complex clusters of individuals and businesses. The centrally integrated bureaucracy has finally fragmented into a constellation of units linked together within a system where boundaries are ambiguously defined and constantly shifting. Within the units, however, amongst suppliers, subcontractors, and so on, traditional hierarchical forms of organisation may persist.

Of course, organisations do not inevitably evolve, step by step, through these six models. As pointed out in earlier chapters, many large corporations remain – despite 'environmental turbulence' – predominantly bureaucratic. Some have experimented with Models 2 and 3 but have been unable to progress further because of a variety of broader environmental factors that generate highly individualistic, competitive attitudes and low-trust working relationships. The transition to a matrix structure (Model 4) – generally regarded as the strongest formal manifestation of 'adhocratic' work relationships – has often proved particularly problematic. Where work complexities and environmental uncertainties are high, matrices offer several potential advantages.

Structuring adhocracy: potential benefits of the matrix

- **Efficiency** Specialised, professional skills are better utilised across complex, open-ended tasks.
- **Flexibility** Swift response to environmental shifts is facilitated by lateral communication channels.
- **Technical excellence** Innovative solutions to complex problems are encouraged by cross-functional collaboration.
- **Balance** Customer needs for project completion and cost control are matched with organisational needs for efficiency and technical capability.
- **Top management** Reduced requirement for senior management intervention in daily operations; more time is available for long-term strategy.
- **Motivation** 'Democracy of expertise' overrides consideration of formal status and motivates members by increasing discretion and teamwork.

In practice, successful implementation of matrix structures often proves extremely difficult. Disputes between organisational members are structured and internalised, rather than removed. Institutionalised conflict between product and function can thus generate personal conflict over, for example, power and recognition. For these reasons matrix structures do not function effectively without mutual trust and confidence. This, in turn, is frequently hampered by the difficulty of achieving a stable balance between function and product/business groups. Conflicts are often resolved by 'tilting the matrix' one way or the other, effectively defeating the purpose of this design. Alternatively, top management may become excessively involved in resolving conflicts between matrix participants. The motivational benefits of matrix structures may also prove illusory. Ambiguously defined tools and conflicting work demands can produce frustration, anxiety and stress. This, in turn, may reduce rather than enhance motivation. Perhaps the most damaging criticism of matrix structures is their tendency to add to administrative costs. In effect professional defensiveness produces more paperwork; increased information flows require more meetings; multiple hierarchies create more managerial overheads. Ironically, then, structural arrangements which are designed to maximise flexibility, innovation and entrepreneurship may actually lead to conflicts and costs which stifle initiatives and demotivate staff. The recent experience of the US computer company, Hewlett Packard, is illustrative.

From adhocracy to bureaucracy: Hewlett Packard

It's amazing that Bob Frankenberg ever got anything done at all. Until last year, the Hewlett-Packard Co. general manager dealt with no fewer than 38 in-house committees. They decided everything from what features to include in a new software program to what city would be best for staging a product launch. Just coming up with a name for the company's New Wave Computing software took nearly 100 people on nine committees seven months. "There was a lot of decision overhead," says John A. Young, HP's chief executive officer.

This is Hewlett-Packard? The company whose blend of advanced technology and enlightened management defined Silicon Valley? The company that year after year topped everybody's list of America's best-managed companies? Could this be the same company whose "HP Way" encouraged innovation by abolishing rigid chains of command, eschewing fancy executive offices, and putting managers, executives, and employees on a first-name basis?

Yes, it's the same old Hewlett-Packard. But by the late 1980s, an unwieldy bureaucracy had bogged down the HP Way. A web of committees, originally designed to foster communication between HP's disparate operating groups, had pushed up costs and slowed down development. . . .

That unwieldy system was developed when HP was trying to move into "open systems" – computers that use non-proprietary software such as American Telephone & Telegraph Co.'s Unix. As it moved to open systems, HP needed to smooth over the differences and update its various computer lines. So it set up a series of committees to figure out what new open-systems technology to pursue, which to ignore, which of HP's products would be saved and which should be shelved. But the committees kept multiplying, like a virus. "Everything was by committee," says Bear, Stearns & Co. analyst Clifford Friedman. "No one could make a decision."

Source: *Business Week*, 1 April, 1991

ORGANISATIONAL STRUCTURE AND MANAGEMENT STYLE

In some cases the difficulties associated with the successful imple-mentation of matrix structures have encouraged many large organ-isations to revert to modified bureaucratic hierarchies. Others have sought to go 'beyond matrix', to project-based and network organisations; included amongst these are corporations which have attempted direct, radical transformations from bureaucratic systems avoiding matrix structures altogether.

But do contemporary network organisations offer greater possibilities for the recreation of the 'small company within the large company'? And how, precisely, do they differ from earlier structural devices designed to encourage flexibility, creativity and responsiveness? To some extent, it is still too early to answer these questions; many networks are too recently established for generalisations to be confidently made. According to one recent observer, however, they may be distinguished from teams, cross-functional task forces and other *ad hoc* structural innovations in three ways.

> First, networks are not temporary. Most task forces assemble to solve a specific problem and then disband and return to business as usual. They do not sustain change in the behaviour of the organisation. Members of a network, on the other hand, identify with it and with each other. . . . Managers' performance and promotability is evaluated with respect to their contribution to the network and sometimes by the network itself.
>
> Second, unlike most teams and task forces, networks do not merely solve problems that have been defined for them. Networks are dynamic; they take initiative . . .
>
> Finally, networks make demands on senior management that teams and task forces do not. CEOs and their direct reports no longer define their jobs as making all substantive operating decisions on their own. Rather their primary job is shaping the processes and personal relationships that allow other managers, the members of the network, to make decisions.
>
> (Charan, 1991, p. 106)

Networks, according to Charan, start from the strategic apex. The chief executive 'must identify the important decision-makers in the organisation, assemble them into a network, and communicate it throughout the company' (ibid., p. 107). Once formed, the network is focused upon 'business fundamentals'. Described in this way, network organisations may be clearly differentiated from task forces, project teams and matrices; in fact, they begin to look rather like streamlined, physically dispersed – but potentially very powerful – committees (Lorenz, 1991).

However, Charan's image of the network organisation is not universally endorsed. Indeed, there remain important differences in the use and application of the network metaphor.

For some commentators, contemporary networks are distinguished by the explicit integration of information technology as an organisation 'design factor', enabling firms to simultaneously increase in size, complexity and responsiveness (Scott Morton, 1991). In this view, IT-facilitated networks are a means for managing both vertical (within function) and lateral (across function, value chain) interdependences. These 'informated' organisations are distinguished by 'considerable interdependence between four domains of managerial activity: intellectual skill development, technology development, strategy formulation, and social system development' (Rockart and Short, 1991, p. 212; Zuboff, 1988). Networked firms are thus seen to be exceptional in the extent to which they are characterised by shared (1) goals; (2) expertise; (3) work; (4) decision-making; (5) timing and issue prioritisation; (6) responsibility, accountability and trust; (7) recognition and reward (Rockart and Short, 1991).

Clearly then, there are substantial variations in the way in which networks are seen to impact existing inter- and intra-organisational relationships. While some discussions focus entirely upon external relationships – joint ventures, strategic alliances and so on – others concentrate upon laterally integrated internal alliances between individuals and teams. Similarly, there are network initiatives which clearly relate to a tightly defined, formally endorsed and relatively permanent cadre; while others seem to loosely involve the majority of organisational members and may form part of wider cultural change programmes designed to promote and extend multiplex, informal relationships.

Given these differences, it is useful to distinguish between three types of network structures – internal, stable and dynamic – each suited to distinct competitive environments (Snow, Miles and Coleman, 1992). (See Figure 8.2)

Internal networks

Internal networks involve the application of market mechanisms to intra-organisational relationships where the corporation continues to

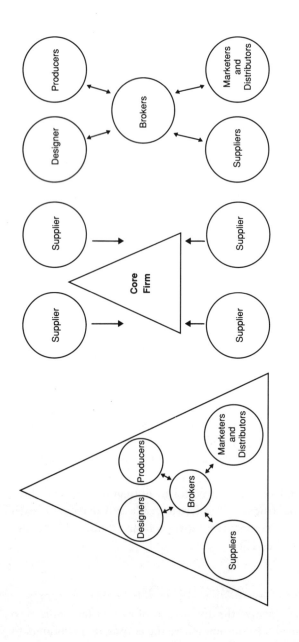

Figure 8.2 Network organisations – a typology

own and control most assets (out-sourcing is limited). Managers in control of corporate assets are 'exposed' to market-related – rather than artificial transfer – prices and, so the argument goes, are thereby encouraged to act in more innovative and entrepreneurial ways. Many large international businesses – aiming to avoid duplication of resources in different countries on the one hand, yet unable to concentrate all resources at the centre or headquarters on the other – have experimented with this form over recent years. One variation of the internal network has recently been developed in General Motors' components business.

An internal network at General Motors

Through a series of reorganizations and consolidations (mostly in the 1980s), GM reduced the number of its components divisions to eight. Each of the eight divisions pursues its own specialty; together, they create what has been called a "specialization consortium."

Turning GM's formerly rigid and inefficient components divisions into a group of co-ordinated and flexible subcontractors required two major actions. First, the parent corporation established clear performance measures for each of the divisions so that their behaviour could be legitimately compared to that of external suppliers. Usually, this meant converting each components facility into a business unit that was encouraged to sell its products on the open market. Second, each division was assigned (or retained) an area of expertise related to a particular automotive system or subassembly. Each division was to be *the* expert at providing its product and to cooperate with other divisions in the consortium whenever appropriate.

To cite a specific example, the AC-Rochester Division was formed in 1988 by merging the former AC Spark Plugs Division and the Rochester Products Division. The combined division specializes in products that govern the flow of air and fluids into and out of the automobile (filters, fuel and exhaust systems, and so forth). The division is organized into several business units, each a specialist, just as AC-Rochester itself is a specialist within the consortium of components divisions. The various business units of AC-Rochester sell their products to GM, of course, but they also sell to Mitsubishi Motors (Japan), Daewoo (Korea), Opel (Europe), and other manufacturers.

Source: Snow, Miles and Coleman (1992, pp. 11–14)

171

Stable networks

By contrast to internal networks, stable networks rely partially upon out-sourcing. The 'core firm' is frequently large and, in terms of its internal organisation, may be relatively bureaucratic. Smaller suppliers produce and supply inputs (often to standards dictated by a strong, centralised technostructure) or distribute outputs. Many large Japanese corporations make extensive use of such networks, claiming advantages in terms of flexibility, risk dispersal and cost reduction. But to ensure stable supplies and maximise co-operation – for quality requirements as well as new product development – parent firms may need to 'look after' their suppliers during economic downturns. In the process, 'independent' suppliers may become excessively dependent and the potential for greater flexibility is significantly reduced. Although sometimes seen as a Japanese model, stable networks have been used by some western companies for many years. Marks and Spencer (see Chapter 6), for example, retails the products of a complex network of manufacturing suppliers with which it deliberately nurtures close, long-term relationships. Stable networks also exist in the car manufacturing industry, as the example of BMW illustrates.

A stable network at BMW

In principle, any part of a BMW is a candidate for outsourcing, and somewhere between 55 and 75 percent of total production costs at BMW come from outsourced parts. As at GM, various internal BMW operating units are obligated to prove their competence according to market standards. Beyond this, however, BMW keeps pace with developments in a variety of relevant product and process technologies through its own subsidiaries, and by partnering with other firms. Three subsidiaries concentrate on technologically advanced forms of automobile development and production: BMW Motor Sports Group, Advanced Engineering Group, and the Motorcycle Group. Each of these subsidiaries, especially Motor Sports and Advanced Engineering, focuses on extending the boundaries of knowledge related to automobile engineering and design. The basic objective of these research groups is to understand enough about a particular technology to know who among potential outside vendors would be the best provider. Further, BMW engages in joint ventures and uses its own venture capital fund to participate financially in the operations of other firms. Currently, four areas are closely monitored: new product materials, new production technologies (e.g., with Cecigram in France), electronics (with Leowe Opta), and basic research in several related fields.

Source: Snow, Miles and Coleman (1992, pp. 13–14)

Dynamic networks

Dynamic networks tend to develop in business environments characterised by rapid and discontinuous change. Consequently, a premium is placed upon specialisation, flexibility and responsiveness, leading to extensive out-sourcing. Indeed, the co-ordinating firm shrinks to a size which, in terms of numbers employed, is sometimes dwarfed by the scale of its producers, suppliers and distributors. The core skill of the co-ordinating firm can vary from manufacturing, to research and development/design or design/assembly. In some cases, it may be a pure brokering role – hence, the 'hollow corporation'. A US review in the mid-1980s discovered networks of this kind in several industrial sectors (See Table 8.1).

Undoubtedly, dynamic networks represent the most dramatic contrast to more conventionally structured organisations. Their appeal lies in the opportunity to focus upon core strengths, reduce

Table 8.1 Dynamic networks: some corporate examples

Company	Products	Revenues ($ millions)	Total employees/ manufacturing employees
Nike	Athletic shoes	1,000	3,500/100
Esprit	Apparel	800	3,000/500
Liz Claiborne	Apparel	570	2,000/250
Emerson Radio	Consumer electronics	500	700/150
TIE	Telecommunications	500	2,100/900
Schwinn Bicycle	Bicycles	150	NA/NA
Sun Microsystems	Computers	150	1,400/200
Lewis Galoob	Toys	58	115/0
Electronic Arts	Software	20	75/0
Ocean Pacific Sunwear	Apparel	15	67/0

(*Source: Business Week*, March 3, 1986, p62)

173

capital requirements and overhead expenses, and facilitate the flexible application of technical and human resources. Perhaps more than any other corporate structure they offer the real prospect of large-scale production through loose confederations of small-scale entrepreneurial units. But the risks are that suppliers may become competitors, control over production (and quality) can be jeopardised and manufacturing/design capabilities can, in effect, be diluted. These considerations have led some to question the long-term durability of network organisations when compared with diversified – but more conventionally integrated – national and multinational corporations.

What, then, are the managerial competencies necessary to sustain and develop network organisations? This question is indirectly addressed in recent discussions of 'entrepreneurship', which have tended to highlight the need for managers to adopt so-called entrepreneurial attributes such as tolerance for risk and individual achievement orientation. But these discussions tend to overlook the fact that, unlike entrepreneurs, corporate managers do not own resources and must work within a complex and partially structured set of relationships with other employees. In this sense, it is inappropriate for managers within network organisations to attempt to behave as classical entrepreneurs, since they must work within and through teams and other colleague coalitions. This aspect is acknowledged by Snow, Miles and Coleman (1992), who distinguish three important 'broker' roles for network managers: architect, lead operator and caretaker.

> [Architects] facilitate the emergence of specific operating networks. . . . A network architect seldom has a clear or complete vision of all the specific operating networks that may ultimately emerge from his or her efforts. . . . The business concept is brought into clearer focus as the broker seeks out firms with desirable expertise, takes an equity position in the firm to coax it into the value chain, helps create new groups that are needed in specialised support roles, and so on. . . . When partners and relationships change frequently, as in dynamic networks, certain managers must devote ongoing effort to the architect's role. . . .
> [Lead operators] take advantage of the groundwork laid by manager-architects . . . (and) formally connect specific firms

together into an operating network . . . the role is often played by a firm positioned downstream in the value chain. Brokers in the lead firm rely on their negotiating and contracting skills to hook together firms into more or less permanent alliances. . . .

[Caretakers] monitor a large number of relationships . . . this means sharing information among firms about how the network runs, as well as information on recent technological and marketing developments, schedules and so on . . . the caretaker does more than help the network plan; managers who play this role also help the network learn.

(Ibid., pp. 15–17)

Together these roles paint a picture of the network manager which is far removed from the figure implied by classical management theory. In the absence of precisely defined hierarchical authority network managers become heavily reliant upon interpersonal skills and lateral influence. Three sets of skills are particularly important. First, the ability to build teams. As allegiances and coalitions shift according to task-related demands, managers must be able to pull individuals together into cohesive teams with a sense of shared purpose. This implies more than simply bringing together the most technically expert individuals; there must also be some sensitivity to the various motives and process contributions which different members bring. Secondly, network managers must be skilful negotiators. Continuously shifting linkages between people, resources and enterprises place a premium upon the ability to make contacts, establish shared interests and 'fix' deals. In this way the network is massaged and manipulated to ensure effective co-ordination within and between teams. Finally, network managers must help others around them to learn. Managerial tasks and problems tend to be non-routine and relatively unstructured; solutions cannot easily be found in already established procedures. As a result, managers must coach, counsel and mentor those around them in the network to routinely learn new ways of working. But who will fill such roles and how will they be developed and rewarded?

STAFFING THE NETWORK ORGANISATION: EMPLOYEES AND THEIR REWARDS

Almost by definition, the core of the network organisation is smaller and flatter than the more conventionally structured corporate hierarchy which it replaces. There is unlikely to be room for extensive ranks of middle managers since the work which they previously supervised directly is now out-sourced and much of the information which they gathered and interpreted may be processed by new technology. Instead, the core is dominated by senior executives with primary responsibility for the formulation and implementation of business strategy; expert professionals responsible for the non-routine development of new products and services; and other technical and administrative staff whose primary function is to allocate, schedule, standardise and co-ordinate work subcontracted to the various parts of the network. In effect, the core is dominated by the strategic apex and the technostructure – with relatively few managerial or support staff. These employees expect high salaries, good working conditions and some measure of security; not, perhaps, lifelong careers but the prospect of adequate compensation if employment is prematurely terminated. Above all, however, they want rewarding work which offers a sense of autonomy, challenge and personal development. Working together in flexible teams they are co-ordinated by a shared sense of purpose or mission, rather than rules and procedures. As such, the primary focus is upon task achievement and high performance, rather than the pursuit of hierarchical position. Appraisal and reward systems are expected to reflect these priorities, as illustrated in the following case.

Appraising performance in a network organisation: Royal Bank of Canada

Royal Bank of Canada has taken the lead in devising new performance metrics that reflect the behavioral imperatives of networks. Top management has developed a one-page statement that specifies the five new criteria by which the bank's top 300 executives will be evaluated. These criteria are crucial ingredients in succession planning and career development. And they are noteworthy precisely because they emphasize behavior and mind-set rather than functional expertise.

Although the document itself must remain confidential, these excerpts suggest the qualities it emphasizes:

A *strong business-profit orientation:* instinctively thinks customer needs, customer service; understands the anatomy of the economic structure of the business; strong innate instincts for making money.

Demonstrate ability to accept accountability, assume leadership and initiative: raises standards constantly as the environment changes; by personality and chemistry, is open and secure in assuming the initiative in building leadership, without horizontal power or authority; believes in sharing information and engendering trust; less control mentality, more empowering mentality; team builder.

Demonstrated record for making a "qualitative shift" and impact on the bank: has shown the vision and courage to change things, not just run things; willingness to experiment.

Astute in the selection of people: demonstrated evidence that this person has the judgment and the security to select and build a team of superior people; willing to cut losses.

Intellectual curiosity and global mind-set: has the mental makeup for learning continuously about global developments, technology, etc. from the outside world.

Royal Bank has also devised an ambitious evaluation program called the "leadership review process" to put these criteria into practice. . . .

First, the manager under review writes a statement of career aspirations and self-appraisal against the performance criteria. Next, the manager submits a list of colleagues to be interviewed by a trusted executive about his or her performance. (Top management's selection of the interviewer is uniquely important; he or she must be widely regarded as honest, apolitical, and seasoned in business judgment.) The list must include at least 7 names (3 peers, 3 subordinates, and 1 boss) but can go as high as 15. The interviews run for an average of one hour and, like the criteria themselves, are meant to be subjective and to focus on behavior. These are not mere note-taking sessions by a human-resource staffer or scripted conversations to rank-order executives along a few obvious dimensions. The interviewer is a savvy, senior-level player with keen insights into other executives. He probes to elicit each individual's opinions and thoughts, always in the context of the business.

Next, the interviewer prepares a one-page profile of the executive's leadership capabilities. this profile, along with the self-assessment, goes for final review to the president and the chairman. In "feed-back sessions," the interviewer discusses the review with the executive and allows him or her to express reservations and reactions.

The leadership review process represents an enormous commitment of time and resources. Indeed, after two years, the bank has still not completed its evaluations of all 200 top executives. But think of its powerful impact on behavior and motivation – even beyond the 200 executives. The dialogue through which top managers devised the performance criteria was itself a valuable learning exercise for them and for everyone who sees the criteria. For the first time, standards of effective behavior have been made visible and concrete. Moreover, the new evaluation system influences the values and behavior of managers interviewed about the performance of their peers and superiors. These managers (many of whom get interviewed about more than one executive) listen to the questions, formulate judgements about individual leadership, decisiveness, and accountability, and become more aware of their own values and behavior in the process. Finally, the promotion of executives based in part on the review – people who might not have been profited under the old system – sends a visible and powerful message throughout the bank about how management values horizontal leadership and behaviors that sustain the network.

Source: Charan (1991, pp. 114–15)

Beyond the core there is a loose federation of different business units variously connected within this and other networks – often with the aid of sophisticated information and telecommunication systems. Satellite organisations may spin off from the core but may remain wholly or partially owned by it. These and other fully independent subcontractors can simply become smaller replicas of the core – with similar organisational structures and relatively privileged employment conditions. Such a pattern may be seen in sectors such as advertising, broadcasting and information technology.

Elsewhere, these peripheral units may concentrate upon the routine production of relatively standardised goods and services – for example, a print unit providing point of sale packaging or a delivery company supplying distribution services. These businesses are more likely to resemble miniature versions of the more formally structured and standardised organisations which were discussed in earlier chapters. Indeed, if a franchise system exists, these are often explicitly designed to recreate a highly standardised formula

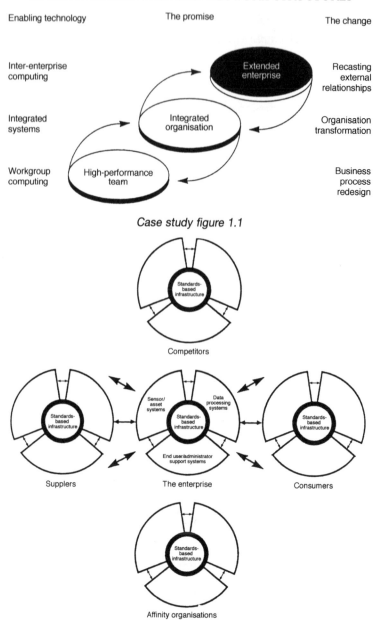

Enabling technology The promise The change

Inter-enterprise computing Extended enterprise Recasting external relationships

Integrated systems Integrated organisation Organisation transformation

Workgroup computing High-performance team Business process redesign

Case study figure 1.1

Competitors

Suppliers The enterprise Consumers

Affinity organisations

Case study figure 1.2
Source: Tapscott and Caston (1993, p. 94)

developed and sold from the core to smaller locally controlled units. In such settings employees may be less skilled, less well paid and less likely to have high-discretion jobs of the kind enjoyed by those in the core. Also in the network will be a heterogeneous collection of very small-scale home-based operations. These may range from highly skilled professionals and executives – complete with high-tech accessories such as personal computers and fax machines – to more traditional craftworkers and relatively unskilled operative and process workers. In terms of work content, material rewards and career profiles, these network members have little in common. Their contract with the core, however, is similar: it involves fees for work completed rather than wages for time spent.

Network structures have the potential to deliver more flexibility to work organisations and more autonomy and choice to individuals. Those with professional, technical and expert skills can construct 'portfolio' and occupational (as distinct from organisational) careers which mix highly demanding, but often very well remunerated, phases in the core with less intensive, less well paid periods else-where in the network. In this way a balance between professional and private life may be achieved, at least over time (Handy, 1990). Some privileged members of the network may, indeed, be able to exercise such choices. But others – the less well educated, members of ethnic minority groups and women, for example – may be permanently trapped in low-skill, low-pay work with little long-term security. This would suggest a growing divide between primary (core) and secondary (periphery) sectors of the labour market with associated implications for rewards systems and career paths. Some networks, it seems, may be characterised by fluid movement of both capital and labour – with new cores constantly growing from smaller units and individuals moving between sectors as skill and knowledge accumulate. Other, more stable networks may remain highly seg-mented with very low rates of mobility.

New technology and the extended enterprise

Just as an enterprise can be viewed as a technology-enabled network of business functions acting as clients and servers, so technology is enabling new client/server networks of enterprises. The *value chain* is becoming a *value network* as enterprises reach out through technology to their customers, suppliers, affinity groups and even competitors (see Case study figures 1.1 and 1.2).

ORGANISATIONAL ISSUES

It is difficult to assess the impact of recent attempts to recreate the entrepreneurial features of smaller-scale organisation within large corporations. Earlier efforts to reintroduce flexibility and responsiveness through matrix structures met with mixed success, excessive formality and complexity being a common problem. More recent, and ambitious, network structures have aimed to loosely integrate individuals and small teams, often within a more market-like set of relationships which are designed to facilitate entrepreneurship. But the linkages may be fragile and the durability of this organisational type is better proven in some forms than in others. Recent experience indicates that within such structures managers may need to fundamentally rethink processes of strategy formulation and implementation as well as develop new models of corporate integration. This implies, in turn, new leadership styles, 'stronger' corporate cultures and the more imaginative application of information technology systems. In addition, there is a need to reconsider the legal, fiscal and organisational implications of what are, in effect, 'boundaryless' organisations. In their most dramatic manifestations, then, networks demand radically different managerial behaviours. Sustaining and reinforcing these behaviours is critical to their long-term viability and represents a major organisational challenge during the 1990s.

While, then, many observers have interpreted current organisational transformations as heralding the end of hierarchy and bureaucracy, our own view is somewhat more cautious. There have been premature announcements of the death of bureaucracy for some thirty years, and the evidence suggests this particular organisational form possesses a remarkable resilience. Indeed, amongst the world's largest and most powerful organisations the predominant 'corporate reality' continues to be bureaucratic. Admittedly, its form and expression may vary – as we have shown in this book – across manufacturing, administrative, consumer service and professional sectors. Within each of these sectors there are organisations which, in turn, are experiencing transitions and transformations in corporate structures, systems and, indeed cultures. But the pace of change should not be exaggerated. Networks are not new. Nor do they transform all organisational forms within them; indeed, they serve to create space for a diverse range of organisations, some of which might otherwise be eliminated. Thus, the network of the modern 'transnational' enterprise may reinvent, in places, the dynamics of the smaller firm – as the excerpts at the beginning of this final chapter suggest. In this sense, modern trends represent a shift towards greater intra-organisational differentiation and fragmentation. The challenge for the 1990s reflects an old organisational dilemma: to balance forces for disintegration with the need for corporate co-ordination and integration, within and across functions, businesses and countries.

BIBLIOGRAPHY

Abbott A. (1988) *The System of Professions: an Essay on the Division of Expert Labour*, Chicago, Ill.: University of Chicago Press.

Bahrami H. (1992) 'The Emerging Flexible Organisation: Perspectives from Silicon Valley', *California Management Review*, Vol. 34, No. 4.

Benveniste G. (1987) *Professionalizing the Organisation: Reducing Bureaucracy to Enhance Effectiveness*, San Francisco, Calif.: Jossey-Bass.

Birley S. and Westhead J. (1990) 'Growth and Performance Contracts Between Types of Small Firms', *Strategic Management Journal*, Vol. 2 No. 2.

Blauner R. (1964) *Alienation and Freedom: the Factory Worker and his Industry*, Chicago, Ill.: University of Chicago Press.

Boddy D., Buchanan D. and Patrickson M. (1991) 'General Insurance' in K. Legge and N. J. Kemp (eds) *Case Studies in Information Technology, People and Organisations*, Oxford: Blackwell.

Braverman H. (1974) *Labour and Monopoly Capital*, New York: Monthly Review Press.

Buchanan D. and McCalman J. (1989) *High Performance Work Systems: the Digital Experience*, London: Routledge.

Burns T. and Stalker G.M. (1961) *The Management of Innovation*, London: Tavistock.

Butler R. (1991) *Designing Organisations*, London: Routledge.

Campbell A. and Gould M. (1987) *Strategies and Styles*, Oxford: Blackwell.

Caulkin S. (1994) 'Confessional for Fallen Professionals', *Observer*, 16 January.

Charan R. (1991) 'How Networks Reshape Organisations – For Results', *Harvard Business Review*, Vol. 69, September–October.

Chell E. (1986) 'The Entrepreneurial Personality; a Review and Some Theoretical Developments', in J. Curran (ed.) *The Survival of the Small Firm* Vol. 2, Aldershot: Gower.

Child J. (1977) *Organization: a Guide to Problems and Practice*, London: Harper and Row.

Clegg S. (1990) *Modern Organisations*, London: Sage.

Crompton R. and Jones G. (1984) *White Collar Proletariat*, London: Macmillan.

Crozier M. (1964) *The Bureaucratic Phenomenon*, Chicago, Ill.: University of Chicago Press.

Davidson M. and Cooper C.L. (1992) *Shattering the Glass Ceiling*, London: Paul Chapman.

Davis H. and Scase R. (forthcoming) *Managing Creativity*, Oxford: Butterworth Heinemann.

Dunne P. and Hughes A. (1990) *Small Businesses: An Analysis of Recent Trends in their Relative Importance and Growth Performance in the UK with Some European Comparisons*, Small Business Research Centre, Working Paper No 1., Department of Applied Economics, Cambridge University.

Edwards R.C. (1979) *Contested Terrain*, London: Heinemann.

Flynn M. (1990) *Public Sector Management*, Hemel Hempstead: Harvester Wheatsheaf.

Fox A. (1974) *Beyond Contract: Work, Power and Trust Relationships*, London: Faber and Faber.

Goffee R. and Scase R. (1985) *Women in Charge*, London: Allen and Unwin.

Goffee R. and Scase R. (1991) 'Proprietorial Control in Family Firms: Some Functions of Quasi-organic Management Systems', *Family Business Review,* Vol. 4 No. 3.

Goldsmith W. and Clutterbuck D. (1985) *The Winning Streak*, Harmondsworth: Penguin.

Goss D. (1991) *Small Business and Society*, London: Routledge.

Gouldner A. (1964) *Patterns of Industrial Bureaucracy*, London: Routledge and Kegan Paul.

Häkansson H. (1989) *Corporate Technological Behaviour: Co-operation and Networks*, London: Routledge.

Hales C. (1993) *Managing through Organisation*, London: Routledge.

Hammer N. and Champy J. (1993) *Re-engineering the Corporation*, London: Nicholas Brealey.

Handy C. (1985) *Understanding Organisations* (3rd edition), Harmondsworth: Penguin.

Handy, C. (1990) *The Age of Unreason*, London: Arrow.

Handy C. (1993) *Understanding Organisations* (4th edition), Harmondsworth: Penguin.

Heskett J.L. (1986) *Managing in the Service Economy*, Boston, Mass.: Harvard Business School Press.

Hirschhorn L. (1988) *The Workplace Within: Psychodynamics of Organisational Life*, Cambridge, Mass.: MIT Press.

Howells D. (1981) 'Marks and Spencer and the Civil Service', *Public Administration*, Autumn.

Hunt J. (1992) *Managing People at Work* (3rd edition), Maidenhead: McGraw-Hill.

Jones P. (ed.) (1989) *Management in Service Industries*, London: Pitman.

Kanter R.M. (1985) *The Change Masters*, London: Unwin.

Kanter R.M. (1989) 'The New Managerial Work', *Harvard Business Review,* Vol. 67 No. 6.

Kanter R.M. (1990) *When Giants Learn to Dance*, London: Unwin.

Keen L. (1994) 'Middle Management Experiences of Devolution', in D.

Adam-Smith and A. Peacock (eds), *Cases in Organisational Behaviour*, London: Pitman.

Kets de Vries M. (1977) 'The Entrepreneurial Personality', *Journal of Management Studies*, Vol. 14, No. 1.

Leadbetter C. (1990) 'Corporate Culture – Shopfloor Transformed', *Financial Times*, 5 January.

Levitt T. (1972) 'Production Line Approach to Service', *Harvard Business Review*, Vol. 50, September–October.

Long R.J. (1987) *New Office Information Technology: Human and Managerial Implications*, London: Croom Helm.

Lorange P. and Roos J. (1993) *Strategic Alliances*, Oxford: Blackwell.

Lorenz C. (1991) 'The Real Meaning of the Networked Organisation', *Financial Times*, 3 April.

Ludlow R. (1987) 'Secure Systems' in S. Tyson and A. Kakabadre (eds) *Cases in Human Resource Management*, London: Heinemann.

McKersie R.B. and Walton R.E. (1991) 'Organisational Change', in M.S. Scott Morton (ed.), *op. cit.*

Meister, D. (1993) *Managing the Professional Service Firm*, Chicago, Ill.: Free Press.

Mintzberg H. (1979) *The Structuring of Organisations*, Englewood Cliffs, N.J.: Prentice Hall.

Mintzberg H., (1983) *Structures in Five*, Englewood Cliffs, N.J.: Prentice Hall.

Morgan G. (1986) *Images of Organisation*, London: Sage.

Morgan G. (1989) *Creative Organization Theory*, London: Sage.

Morgan J. (1986) 'The BBC and the Concept of Public Sector Broadcasting' in C. MacCabe and O. Stewart (eds) *The BBC and Public Service Broadcasting*, Manchester: Manchester University Press.

Nat West Quarterly Survey of Small Businesses, Vol. 6 No. 2 (1990)

Perrow C. (1979) *Complex Organisations: A Critical Essay* (2nd edition) Dallas: Scott, Foresman.

Peters T. (1992) *Liberation Management*, London: Pan Macmillan.

Peters T. and Austin N. (1986) *A Passion For Excellence: the Leadership Difference*, Glasgow: Fontana Collins.

Peters T. and Waterman R. (1982) *In Search of Excellence*, New York: Harper and Row.

Pfeffer J. (1994) *Competitive Advantage Through People: Unleashing the Power of the Workforce*, Boston, Mass.: Harvard Business School Press.

Podmore D. and Spencer A. (1987) *In a Man's World: Essays on Women in Male Dominated Professions*, London: Tavistock.

Pugh D. (1979) *Writers on Organizations*, Harmondsworth: Penguin.

Rockart J.F. and Short J.E. (1991) 'The Networked Organisation and the Management of Interdependence' in M.S. Scott Morton (ed.) *op. cit.*

Sabel C.F. (1982) *Work and Politics and the Division of Labour in Industry*, Cambridge: Cambridge University Press.

Salaman, G. (1977) 'An Historical Discontinuity: From Charisma to Routinization', *Humnan Resources*, No. 30 (1977).

Scase R. (1991) 'The New Organisation', *Financial Times*, 25 November.

Scase R. (1995) 'Industrial Relations in Small Firms', in P. Edwards (ed.) *Industrial Relations in Britain*. (2nd edition), London: Macmillan.

Scase R. and Goffee R. (1982) *The Entrepreneurial Middle Class*, London: Croom Helm.

Scase R. and Goffee R. (1987a) *The Real World of the Small Business Owner* (2nd edition), London: Routledge.

Scase R. and Goffee R. (1987b) 'Why Managers Turn Entrepreneur', *Management Today*, August.

Scase R. and Goffee R. (1989) *Reluctant Managers*, London: Routledge.

Scott Morton M.S. (ed.) (1991) *The Corporation of the 1990s: Information Technology and Organizational Transformation*, New York: Oxford University Press.

Sieff M. (1988) *Don't Ask the Price*, London: Fontana.

Slatter S. (1992) *Gambling on Growth*, Chichester: Wiley.

Snow C.C., Miles R.E. and Coleman H.J. (1992) 'Managing Twenty First Century Network Organisations', *Organizational Dynamics*, Winter, pp. 5–20.

Sofer C. (1973) *Organizations in Theory and Practice*, London: Heinemann.

Sparks L. (1989) 'The Retail Sector' in P. Jones (ed.) *Management in Service Industries*, London: Pitman.

Stewart R. (1991) *Managing Today and Tomorrow*, London: Macmillan.

Swieringa J. and Wierdsma A. (1992) *Becoming a Learning Organisation – Beyond the Learning Curve*, Reading, Mass.: Addison Wesley.

Tapscott D. and Caston A. (1993) *Paradigm Shift: the New Promise of Information and Technology*, New York: McGraw-Hill

Toffler A. (1985) *The Adaptive Corporation*, London: Pan.

Trompenaars F. (1993) *Riding the Waves of Culture*, London: Economist Books.

Weber M. (1964) *The Theory of Economic and Social Organisation*, New York: Free Press.

Wessner K.W. (1981)'A Company needs Vision as well as Controls', *Management Review*, Vol. 70.

Wickens P. (1987) *The Road to Nissan*, London: Macmillan.

Willman P., (1989) 'Human Resource Management in the Service Sector', in P. Jones (ed.) *op. cit.*

Wilson D. and Rosenfeld R. (1990) *Managing Organisations*, Maidenhead: McGraw Hill.

Wood S. (1989) 'The Transformation of Work?' in S. Wood (ed.) *The Transformation of Work?*, London: Unwin Hyman.

Zuboff S. (1988) *In the Age of the Smart Machine*, London: Heinemann.

INDEX